HISPANIC-AMERICAN SCIENTISTS

WALTER OLEKSY

☑®
Facts On File, Inc.

To tomorrow's achievers:
Ryan and Karen Emerson
Justin and Kaitlyn Lee Ohde
Alex, Natalie, and Matthew Schmidt
Chris and Jon Yabiku

American Profiles: Hispanic-American Scientists

Copyright © 1998 by Walter Oleksy

Facts On File, Inc.
11 Penn Plaza
New York NY 10001

Library of Congress Cataloging-in-Publication Data

Oleksy, Walter G., 1930–
    Hispanic-American scientists / Walter Oleksy.
        p.   cm.—(American profiles)
    Includes bibliographical references and index.
    ISBN 0-8160-3704-3
    1. Hispanic American scientists—Biography. 2. Hispanic American engineers—Biography. 3. Scientists—United States—Biography. 4. Engineers—United States—Biography. I. Title. II. Series: American profiles (Facts on File, Inc.)
    Q141.042   1998
    508.968'073—dc21   98-6558

Facts On File books are available at special discounts when purchased in bulk quantities for businesses, associations, institutions or sales promotions. Please call our Special Sales Department in New York at 212/967-8800 or 800/322-8755.

You can find Facts On File on the World Wide Web at http://www.factsonfile.com

Text design by Cathy Rincon
Cover design by Matt Galemmo

Printed in the United States of America.

MP FOF 10 9 8 7 6 5 4 3 2

This book is printed on acid-free paper.

Contents

Introduction   v

LUIS ALVAREZ   1
Physicist (1911–1988)

DAVID CARDUS   13
Physician (1922–)

MANUEL CARDONA   23
Physicist (1934–)

PEDRO SANCHEZ   33
Soil Scientist (1940–)

MARIO MOLINA   45
Environmental Chemist (1943–)

HENRY DIAZ   56
Meteorologist (1948–)

FRANCISCO DALLMEIER 69
Wildlife Biologist (1953–)

ADRIANA OCAMPO 83
Planetary Geologist (1955–)

MARGARITA COLMENARES 95
Environmental Engineer (1957–)

ELLEN OCHOA: 107
Electrical Engineer and
Astronaut (1958–)

Index 117

Introduction

Hispanics are a greatly diverse and talented people. Their cultural ties are to Mexico, the Caribbean countries, Central America, South America, or Spain. Over the years, many Hispanics have immigrated to the United States, mainly for political, educational, or economic reasons.

More than 100 years ago, the American poet Walt Whitman (1819–92) said that there is much of importance about the Latin contributions to American nationality that may never be put on the record. Since then this overlooking of talent has been increasingly corrected as Americans learn of and recognize the many men and women of Hispanic birth or ancestry who have made and are making important contributions to U.S. society and the world as artists, writers, musicians, athletes, scientists, and other professionals.

This book describes the lives and careers of 10 Hispanic-American scientists whose achievements in fields such as physics, biology, chemistry, meteorology, geology, medicine, environmental engineering, soil science, optics, and space exploration have occurred since the end of World War II.

Several of these Hispanic-American scientists are Nobel Prize winners. The Nobel Prize is given annually for outstanding achievement in physics, chemistry, physiology or medicine, economics, literature, and peace. First given in 1901, the awards were established by the will of Alfred Nobel, Swedish chemist and inventor of dynamite, as a humanitarian and peace-promoting gesture.

Space limitations have prevented others from being included. A sampling follows.

- Dr. Franklin Chang-Díaz, the first Latino astronaut, a veteran of four space flights. In 1993 he was appointed director of the Advanced Space Propulsion Laboratory at the Johnson Space Center in Houston, Texas, where he continues his research on plasma rockets.
- Dr. Antonia Novello, Puerto Rican–born, the first Hispanic and first woman to become U.S. surgeon general, the nation's chief doctor.
- Jaime Escalante, Bolivian-born, one of the United States's most notable mathematics and science teachers, his work was dramatized in the 1988 movie *Stand and Deliver.*
- Albert Baez, Mexican-born physicist, who conducted pioneering work with X rays that laid foundations for the science of X-ray imaging optics.
- Orlando Gutiérrez, Cuban-born engineer, who works in thermodynamics and aeroacoustics.
- Richard Tapia, of Mexican ancestry, a nationally recognized leader in minority education in mathematics.
- Juan Carlos Romero, Argentine-born authority on the physiology of the kidney and its relationship to the development of high blood pressure.

In this book, the 10 American scientists whom the reader will meet were either born in Latin countries or are of Hispanic descent and are among the most important achievers in their fields. Most of those who were born in other countries came to the United States for political freedom or educational opportunities that they hoped to find there. Most said that their Hispanic backgrounds and knowledge of Spanish helped them in their careers. All those still living took time out of their busy lives and careers to be interviewed by the author for this book. The author wishes to thank them for their enthusiastic cooperation.

Luis Alvarez won a Nobel Prize in physics for work with a liquid hydrogen bubble chamber that greatly expanded the list of known subnuclear particles. (Courtesy Lawrence Berkeley National Laboratory)

Luis Alvarez

PHYSICIST
(1911–1988)

Luis Alvarez, Hispanic-American Nobel Prize–winning physicist, was among a small group of scientists aboard the *Enola Gay* on August 6, 1945. This was the United States's B-29 bomber that dropped the first atomic bomb on a populated area. Alvarez's job was to monitor the energy of the explosion over the Japanese city of Hiroshima when the bomb was dropped.

"My first sensation was one of intense light covering my whole field of vision," he wrote years later in his autobiography, *Alvarez: Adventures of a Physicist,* describing what he saw and felt as he watched the explosion from the plane high above the city.

> This seemed to last for about half a second, after which I noted an intense orange-red glow through the clouds. Several seconds later it seemed that a second spherical red ball appeared, but it is probable that this phenomenon was caused by the motion of the airplane bringing us to a position where we could see through

the cloud directly at the ball of fire which had been developing for the past few seconds.

In about eight minutes the top of the cloud was at approximately 40,000 feet (12 km), as close as I could estimate from our altitude of 24,000 feet (7 km), and this seemed to be the maximum altitude attained by the cloud.

I did not feel the shock wave hit the plane, but the pilot felt the reaction of the rudder through the rudder pedals. Some of the other passengers in the plane noted a rather small shock at the time, but it was not apparent to me.

The blast killed or injured almost 130,000 people, and 90 percent of the city of Hiroshima was leveled.

After the bombing, Alvarez wrote a letter to his son Walter, then four years old, describing his thoughts about the consequences of the bombing he had just witnessed:

What regrets I have about being a party to killing and maiming thousands of Japanese civilians this morning are tempered with the hope that this terrible weapon we have created may bring the countries of the world together and prevent further wars. Alfred Nobel, the Swedish inventor of dynamite, thought that his invention of high explosives would have that effect, by making wars too terrible, but unfortunately it had just the opposite reaction. Our new destructive force is so many thousands of times worse that it may realize Nobel's dream.

Three days later, another atomic bomb was dropped, this one on the city of Nagasaki, killing or wounding 75,000 people. Shortly afterward, the Japanese government sued for peace, ending World War II in the Pacific.

During the war, besides helping create the world's first nuclear weapons, Alvarez developed a narrow beam radar system that allowed airplanes to land in inclement weather. After the war, he worked on a theory that a massive collision of a meteorite with Earth 65 million years ago brought about the extinction of dinosaurs. In 1968 he won the Nobel Prize for physics for his development of giant bubble chambers used to detect a variety of subatomic particles.

☆ ☆ ☆

Luis Walter Alvarez was born on June 13, 1911, in San Francisco, California, of Spanish and Cuban descent. His father, Walter Clement Alvarez, was a doctor in private practice and also a medical researcher at the University of California at San Francisco. His paternal grandfather, Walter Alvarez, was born in Spain but moved to Cuba and then emigrated to the United States where he became wealthy as an owner of real estate in Los Angeles, California. Luis Alvarez's mother was Harriet Skidmore Smythe Alvarez. His mother's family came to the United States from Ireland and established a missionary school in China. His parents met while studying at the University of California at Berkeley, which later became his own base of teaching and research.

Alvarez attended grammar school in San Francisco and afterward enrolled in the city's Polytechnic High School where he excelled in science. When his father joined the staff of the Mayo Clinic, the family moved to Rochester, Minnesota, and Alvarez then studied at Rochester High School. Alvarez's father noticed his son's growing interest in physics and hired another Mayo staffer to give him private lessons on weekends.

Planning to major in organic chemistry, Alvarez enrolled at the University of Chicago in 1928 but came to dislike the mandatory chemistry laboratory study. In his junior year, he took a laboratory course entitled "Advanced Experimental Physics: Light." "It was love at first sight," he later wrote in his autobiography. He changed his major to physics and received his bachelor of science degree in 1932. During his undergraduate years, Alvarez was a member of Phi Gamma Delta fraternity and lived in the frat house, which he said was "the center of my social life."

Staying at Chicago for his graduate work, his advisor was Nobel Laureate Arthur Compton. Alvarez liked Compton because "He visited my laboratory only once during my graduate career and usually had no idea how I was spending my time." Most of it was spent at the school library and, after moving out of the Phi Gamma Delta house and joining the Gamma Alpha graduate scientific fraternity, playing bridge or the piano at Gamma Alpha's frat house. He also took up the sports of ballooning and parachute jumping and learned to fly an airplane.

Alvarez's time was also spent dating Geraldine Smithwick, a very pretty and popular senior in college. They met on a double date and soon afterward began dating steadily. Shortly before receiving his doctorate in physics at the University of Chicago in 1936, Alvarez and Smithwick married. They later had two children, Walter and Jean.

Less than a month after his wedding and graduation, Alvarez joined the faculty of the University of California at Berkeley. There he became a research scientist with Nobel Prize–winning physicist Ernest Orlando Lawrence, who became his mentor. Alvarez's association with the University of California continued for 42 years until his retirement in 1978.

Soon after arriving at Berkeley, Alvarez's colleagues began calling him the "prize wild idea man" because of his involvement in a wide range of research projects. Many of them had to do with atomic energy and the structure of an atom. Atomic energy is the enormous energy released by rearrangements—splitting or fusing—of atomic nuclei, such as the energy in an atomic bomb.

An atom is the smallest component of a chemical element that still has all the properties of that element. It consists of a positively charged central core, the nucleus, surrounded by one or more negatively charged particles called electrons. Almost all the mass of the atom resides in the nucleus, which is composed of two different types of stable particle of almost equal mass—the proton, which is positively charged, and the neutron, which is electrically neutral.

During Alvarez's first year at Berkeley, he discovered the process of K-electron capture. It is the process in which an atomic nucleus absorbs an electron from the innermost shell (the K-shell) of its orbital (circulating) electrons, thus transforming into another nuclide (a nucleus with a given number of combined protons and neutrons).

Also, with a student named Jake Wiens, Alvarez developed a mercury vapor lamp whose wavelength (motion fluctuation) was adopted as an official standard of length by the U.S. Bureau of Standards.

Just after the outbreak of World War II in Europe (1939), Alvarez discovered tritium, a radioactive isotope (a variant atom containing a different number of protons) of hydrogen.

As World War II spread across Europe in 1940 and the United States prepared for possible entry into the conflict, Alvarez began research for the military at the Massachusetts Institute of Technology (MIT) in Cambridge. On various "on-loan" assignments over the next five years, Alvarez collaborated in the development of radar (Radio Detecting And Ranging) systems. He developed a very narrow radar beam to allow a ground-based controller to direct the "blind" landing of an airplane in inclement weather. He also developed a method for locating and bombing objects on the ground when they could not be seen by a pilot. A third invention became known as the microwave early-warning system, a mechanism for collecting images of aircraft movement in overcast skies. All three discoveries played important parts in the safety and accuracy of American and Allied bombing missions, which resulted in their supremacy over the skies in World War II.

Alvarez was given an even more important assignment in 1943. He joined the staff of physicist Enrico Fermi at Argonne Laboratories outside Chicago, Illinois. Fermi had won the 1938 Nobel Prize in physics; in 1942 he created the first self-sustaining nuclear chain reaction in uranium. After six months of working with Fermi at Argonne, Alvarez was assigned to the top-secret work that was called the Manhattan Project. He was to conduct research on development of the atomic bomb at Los Alamos, New Mexico.

Alvarez's primary accomplishment with the Manhattan Project team was developing the detonating device used for the first plutonium bomb (one of two types of early atomic bombs). He flew in the B-29 bomber that observed the first test of an atomic device at Alamogordo, south of Los Alamos. Three weeks later, he was aboard the *Enola Gay* as it dropped the atomic bomb on Hiroshima.

Like most other scientists working on the atomic bomb, Alvarez was horrified by the destruction of the weapon that he had helped to create. But he had supported its use in order to hasten an end to the

Alvarez's discoveries with the bubble chamber, "Entirely new possibilities for research into high-energy physics present themselves. Practically all the discoveries made in this important field [of particle physics] were possible only through the use of methods developed by Professor Alvarez."

By this time Alvarez and his wife had divorced, largely as a result of being separated during his war-related work. He attended the Nobel ceremony with his second wife, Janet Landis, whom he had married in 1958. With her, Alvarez had two more children, Donald and Helen.

A few years earlier, in late 1963, Alvarez again served his country under circumstances far different from the war: He assisted in the investigation of the assassination of President John F. Kennedy. Alvarez was asked to study several hundred photographs of the shooting to help determine where the bullet that killed the president came from and the exact time at which it was fired. Although he disagreed with others on some technical aspects of these matters, he agreed with those who believed Lee Harvey Oswald shot Kennedy and had acted alone in the killing.

In 1965, Alvarez's interests turned from scientific curiosity about atomic particles to interest in the past. He led a joint Egyptian-American expedition to search for hidden chambers in the pyramid of King Kefren at Giza in Egypt. The team focused high-energy muons (subatomic particles produced by cosmic rays) at the pyramid to look for areas of low density, which could indicate possible chambers; however, none were found.

In 1980, again researching into the past, Alvarez and his son Walter, by then a professor of geology at Berkeley, were on an expedition in Italy when they accidentally discovered a band of sedimentary rock that contained an unusually high level of the rare metal iridium. Using dating techniques, they estimated that the rock was about 65 million years old.

This led them to hypothesize that the iridium came from an asteroid that had struck Earth and then sent huge volumes of smoke and dust, including the iridium, into the Earth's atmosphere. The dense cloud may have shut out sunlight for an extended period of time and could have caused the widespread death of plant life on

Alvarez (right) at the Berkeley National Laboratory with colleagues (from left) Helen Michel, Frank Asaro, and his son Walter Alvarez (Courtesy Lawrence Berkeley National Laboratory)

Earth. The loss of plant life could then have brought about the extinction of dinosaurs who fed on the plants. Their theory remains controversial, and while many scientists support it, there are many others who do not.

Alvarez's scientific interests remained varied throughout his career. Among his inventions were a system for color television and an electronic indoor golf training device he developed for President Dwight D. Eisenhower. In all, Alvarez held 22 patents for his inventions.

The question of whether atomic bombs should have been dropped on the Japanese to end World War II was asked of Alvarez all his life, but he had made peace with himself regarding his

*A*ll *the scientists I know are trained to ask "Why?" continually.*

—Luis Alvarez

role in developing the bomb and its use. In his autobiography in 1987 Alvarez wrote:

> I have to express sorrow at the terrible loss of life on both sides in that last world war . . . I believe that the present stability of the world rests primarily on the existence of nuclear weapons, a Pandora's box I helped open with my tritium work and at Los Alamos. I believe nuclear weapons have persuaded the two superpowers [the United States and the Soviet Union] to work together to defuse dangerous international conflicts.
>
> I'm happy that we apparently have broken the twenty-five year cycle of European wars, two of which enlarged to world wars. I had something to do with this seminal change in the direction of world affairs. I feel great pride in that accomplishment.
>
> I'm very much in favor of the eventual elimination of *all* weapons, both nuclear and conventional, though I doubt that anyone alive will see the day when that happens. It will take, I would guess, about a hundred years to come to so utopian a condition.

Alvarez did not live to see the dissolution of the Soviet Union in 1991 and the subsequent lessening threat of nuclear war. He died of cancer in Berkeley on September 1, 1988, a year after publication of his autobiography.

Chronology

JUNE 13, 1911	Luis Walter Alvarez is born in San Francisco, California
1932	receives bachelor of science degree in physics from University of Chicago
1933	receives master's degree in physics from University of Chicago
1936	marries Geraldine Smithwick; receives doctorate degree in physics from Univer-

1940	discovers the radioactive isotope tritium
1940–43	conducts radar research at Massachusetts Institute of Technology
1943	joins Enrico Fermi staff at Argonne Laboratories, Chicago; conducts atomic bomb research at Los Alamos, New Mexico
1945	is research scientist aboard plane that drops atomic bomb on Hiroshima; returns to University of California at Berkeley as professor of physics
1950–59	conducts research on atomic particles; is divorced
1958	marries Janet Landis
1963	investigates John F. Kennedy assassination
1965	goes to Egypt to study burial chambers in pyramid of King Kefren
1968	is awarded Nobel Prize in physics
1978	retires from University of California at Berkeley
1980	theorizes why dinosaurs became extinct
SEPTEMBER 1, 1988	Luis Alvarez dies of cancer in Berkeley, California

sity of Chicago; joins physics faculty of University of California at Berkeley

Further Reading

Book By Luis Alvarez

Alvarez, Luis W. *Alvarez: Adventures of a Physicist.* New York: Basic Books, 1987. Comprehensive, at times exciting autobiography.

Books about Luis Alvarez

Daintith, John, ed. *A Biographical Encyclopedia of Scientists.* New York: Facts On File, 1981. Brief biography of Luis Alvarez.

McGraw-Hill. *Modern Scientists and Engineers.* New York: McGraw-Hill, 1980. Brief biography of Alvarez.

McMurray, Emily J. *Notable Twentieth-Century Scientists.* Detroit: Gale, 1995. Brief biography of Alvarez.

Weber, Robert L. *Pioneers of Science: Nobel Prize Winners in Physics.* New York: American Institute of Physics, 1980.

Books on Related Topics

Black, Walace B. *Hiroshima and the Atomic Bomb.* New York: Crestwood House, 1993. A book for young people that clearly explains creation of the atomic bomb and its detonation on Hiroshima.

Kerrod, Robin. *The Simon & Schuster Young Readers' Book of Science.* New York: Simon & Schuster, 1991. A good introduction to physics for preteens and teenagers.

Van Cleave, Janice Pratt. *Janice Van Cleave's 101 Easy Experiments in Motion, Heat, Light, Machines, and Sound.* New York: Wiley, 1991. A clearly written introduction to the laws of physics for young people.

David Cardús

PHYSICIAN
(1922–   )

On July 20, 1969, mission control at the National Aeronautics and Space Administration (NASA) in Houston, Texas, received a message from the Moon: "Houston, Tranquility base here. The Eagle has landed." America's space program had astonished the world by successfully putting two astronauts, Neil Armstrong and Edwin Aldrin Jr., on the Moon some 238,000 miles (383 km) into space.

"That was one of the most exciting moments in my career and my life," said Dr. David Cardús, a Spanish-born American physician. "Although my contribution to the Moon landing was small, I was excited because I had participated in the physiological studies that led to the selection of America's first astronauts. I felt that I was a part of history and it was a very exciting time for me."

☆ ☆ ☆

David Cardús, a physician specializing in cardiology and biomathematics, conducted physical examinations on America's first astronauts and is a leading researcher in the use of computers and other technology in medicine. (Courtesy Baylor College of Medicine)

David Cardús was born on August 6, 1922, in Barcelona, Spain, to Jaume and Ferranda Pascual Cardús. He went to primary school in Barcelona until the age of 10; then he attended the Institut-Escola in that city.

"It was an innovative school where studies of primary and secondary education were combined," Cardús recalled in an interview. "Students had a great responsibility in choosing their own studies in sciences, humanities, arts, and also in some manual professions under the guidance of their teachers."

Cardús began studying at the Institut-Escola in 1932. A year later, his mother died. Cardús graduated from the school in 1938, and a year later, as Spain was engulfed in civil war, his father was exiled to France. Cardús followed him there.

"In France, I had the opportunity to enter the University of Montpellier," said Cardús. "I had to take physics, chemistry, and biology courses again because my studies in Spain were during the dictatorship of General Francisco Franco and were all invalidated." Cardús received his bachelor of arts and sciences degree from the University of Montpellier in 1942.

"I lived in France with my father until I graduated," Cardús said.

> Then I had to present myself to the Spanish authorities in order to initiate my military service. I presented myself to the military authorities in Spain and learned that no documentation on me had arrived yet from the Spanish consulate in France.
>
> Spanish authorities did not have my college records, so they considered me a draft evader, and I was not allowed to leave my living quarters. Police visited me everyday for several months to make sure I didn't run away. Meanwhile, authorities debated whether [or not] to send me to a disciplinary battalion in Africa. Finally, my documents arrived from France, and I was assigned to serve in Spain's regular army.

After four years of military service, Cardús was released and began studying medicine at the Medical School of the University of Barcelona. He earned an M.D. degree in 1949, graduating *magna cum laude.*

Cardús did his internship at the Hospital Clínico of the University of Barcelona from 1949 to 1950, and his residency in respiratory diseases, at the Sanatorio del Puig d'Olena in Barcelona from 1950 to 1953. During this period, in 1951, Cardús married Francesca Ribas, and the couple have since had four children.

At the end of his internship, Cardús accepted a two-year research fellowship in cardiology from the French government and did postgraduate work in the departments of cardiology at two hospitals in Paris. Cardiology is the study of the heart and its functions in health and disease. Afterward, Cardús returned to the University of Barcelona and received his diploma in cardiology from the Postgraduate School of Cardiology in 1956.

Next, Cardús moved on to Manchester, England, having accepted a British research fellowship at the University of Manchester's Royal Infirmary. In 1957 he left Europe to take up residence in the United States and became a research associate at the Lovelace Foundation in Albuquerque, New Mexico.

After three years, Cardús began a long association with the Institute for Rehabilitation and Research at Baylor College of Medicine in Houston, Texas. Over the years, he has served on the medical staff as a professor in the rehabilitation and physiology departments, as director of the biomathematics division, and as head of the exercise and cardiopulmonary laboratories. He also has taught mathematical sciences and statistics at Rice University in Houston for many years and served as a consultant to the U.S. Public Health Service in the planning of health facilities.

Cardús has made a name for himself in various fields of medicine including the United States's space program. His major areas of medical interest are cardiology, gravitational physiology, preventative medicine, spinal injury rehabilitation, and the human aging

> *T*ake every opportunity to gain knowledge. Knowledge is at the basis of the decisions that prepare us to confront the problems of life and that set us free.
>
> —David Cardús

process. His work with mathematical and computer applications for the study of physiological systems and his research on experimental exercise and respiratory physiology signify not only the general introduction of computer technology to medical science but also a major contribution to physical and physiological studies of astronauts and paraplegics.

His major points of research include exercise physiology as applied to space research, health, and aging, and rehabilitation medicine as applied to cardiac rehabilitation, bladder dynamics, and body composition in extensive paralysis. He also has been a leader in the application of computers and mathematical models to medicine and applying costs to benefits in rehabilitation medicine.

> M*y career as a doctor has given me access to the human being in ways I would not otherwise have had. It's helped me to better understand people and the complex problems that are part of social life.*
>
> —David Cardús

It was back in an early phase of his career, however, that Cardús conducted research that led him to participate in the physical health aspects of America's space program. He spent several years studying many new scientific and medical technologies involving the measurement of human health and fitness. He combined this knowledge with a use of statistics and was then able to computerize the study of exercise physiology. New methodological developments resulting from these studies brought him into the U.S. space program at the Lovelace Foundation in Albuquerque, New Mexico, in 1951 as a research associate. "I conducted studies that led to the selection of the first seven astronauts out of 66 pilots that had been chosen from different branches of the armed forces," Cardús recalled.

Cardús has continued research in the U.S. space program in the field of artificial gravity by conducting experiments with a centrifuge he designed that is presently located at the NASA Johnson Space Center in Houston. A centrifuge is an apparatus that rotates at high

Cardús with the artificial gravity simulator he designed for the National Aeronautics and Space Administration, used in astronaut space training (Courtesy Baylor College of Medicine)

speed and separates substances of different densities, such as milk and cream.

On another front, in an extended application of the principles of exercise physiology, Cardús created in 1965 the first cardiac rehabilitation program in Houston in the Department of Rehabilitation of Baylor College of Medicine. The American Heart Association established its Work Evaluation Unit of Houston in Cardús's laboratory.

A further extension of the methods of testing developed for cardiac patients were adapted for studies of the cardiovascular condition of paraplegics, patients with spinal cord injury that renders them paralyzed from the waist down. The application of the principles of exercise physiology to cardiac and spinal cord injury patients were instrumental in a number of research projects where the aging effects on physical condition were studied in those two areas.

Cardús's contributions resulting from mathematical and computer applications have consisted of the transforming of biological data into computer software for the automatic processing of information about the functioning and health of the body. Parts of his course of biomathematics for medical and graduate students at Baylor College of Medicine have been incorporated into the curriculum of the Department of Mathematical Sciences at Rice University. And to the subject Cardús has also contributed a book, *An Introduction to Mathematics for Physicians and Biologists.* Finally, in collaboration with Dr. William A. Spencer he was influential in the introduction of computers to the Texas Medical Center in the early 1960s.

Another aspect of Cardús's mathematical work relates to the application of benefit-cost theory to rehabilitation medicine. This work resulted in two mathematical-computer models for assisting decision makers in the selection of proposed rehabilitation research and in the managed allocation of resources of the federal and state rehabilitation programs.

Cardús has conducted research and written many reports on rehabilitation for heart disease patients and those recovering from spinal cord injuries, much of it involving use of computer technology. In fact in 1972, he was honored with a gold medal from the International Congress of Physical Medicine and Rehabilitation for having demonstrated the use of computers, video, and telecommunications in physical rehabilitation.

"I had not developed the technology," said Cardús,

> but followed it very closely and was able to create a demonstration that showed it was potentially useful for medicine and mankind. The demonstration involved what today is called telemedicine. My colleagues and I set up demonstrations, which I believe were the first of their kind to show the usefulness of computers and telecommunications in medicine.

The exhibit consisted of sending medical data generated by an individual doing an exercise test in Barcelona to Cardús's lab in Houston. Doctors and researchers could see a patient doing exercises in their presence and how the variables resulting were recorded, calculated, and displayed on a large screen in a receiving room in Barcelona. According to Cardús:

> The demonstration was a result of the combined resources of IBM and the telephone companies and Western Union in the

United States and Barcelona. Its success was mentioned in all the important press in many parts of Europe.

This was indeed a technological demonstration of the capabilities of computers and telecommunications in medicine. Since then the technology has made it possible for patients living in remote locations to have the aid of medical experts anywhere in the world.

Cardús is active in many medical and other professional societies including the American Congress of Physical Medicine and Rehabilitation, the American Physiological Society, the American Association for the Advancement of Science, the American College of Cardiology, the American Heart Association, and the Aerospace Medical Association. He was president of the International Society for Gravitational Physiology in 1993 and vice chairman of the Gordon Conference on Biomathematics in 1970. He also has served as chairman of the board of the Institute for Hispanic Culture in Houston and as president of Spanish Professionals in America.

In 1993 Cardús became president of the International Society for Gravitational Physiology. That same year he received an honorary doctor's degree from the Universitat de Barcelona.

In 1994 Cardús became a member of the editorial board of the *Journal of Gravitational Physiology*. In 1996 he was given the Joan d'Alòs award from the Centre Cardiovascular Sant Jordi, Barcelona, Spain.

Cardús has been honored with numerous other awards from professional organizations both in the United States and Spain. He has received first prizes from the International American Congress of Rehabilitative Medicine and the American Urological Association for creation of several exhibits. He also was given an award for science writing from the American Congress of Physical Medicine and Rehabilitation.

Cardús became a United States citizen in 1969. When asked if his Hispanic background helped or hindered his career, he replied, "America is a very open country. From the first day I arrived in the United States I felt I was equal to others in the pursuit of my profession. I found no prejudice here."

Chronology

AUGUST 6, 1922	David Cardús is born in Barcelona, Spain
1942	receives bachelor of science degree from University of Montpellier, France
1949	receives doctor of medicine degree from University of Barcelona
1949–53	completes internship at Hospital Clínico, University of Barcelona, and residency at Sanatorio del Puig d'Olena in Barcelona; marries Francesca Ribas
1953	accepts French fellowship in cardiology in Paris
1956	receives diploma in cardiology at University of Barcelona
1957	accepts British fellowship at University of Manchester's Royal Infirmary; becomes research associate at Lovelace Foundation in Albuquerque, New Mexico
1960	joins medical staff of Institute for Rehabilitation and Research at Baylor College of Medicine in Houston, Texas
1969	becomes professor in department of rehabilitation at Baylor; becomes U.S. citizen
1973	becomes professor in department of physiology at Baylor
1993	becomes president of International Society for Gravitational Physiology; receives honorary doctorate from Universitat de Barcelona
1994	becomes a member of editorial board of *Journal of Gravitational Physiology*

| 1996 | is given the Joan d'Alòs award from the Centre Cardiovascular Sant Jordi, Barcelona, Spain |

Further Reading

Book about David Cardús

McMurray, Emily J. *Notable Twentieth-Century Scientists.* Detroit: Gale, 1995. Brief biography of Cardús.

Books on Related Topics

Dinn, Sheila. *Hearts of Gold: A Celebration of Special Olympics and Its Heroes.* Woodbridge, Conn.: Blackbirch Press, 1996. A book that tells young readers about boys and girls who are living with their physical or emotional handicaps.

Hoffa, Helynn, and Gary Morgan. *Yes You Can: A Helpbook for the Physically Disabled.* New York: Pharos Books, 1990. Good background book on how those who are physically disabled can live a more normal life.

Oleksy, Walter. *The Information Revolution in Science and Medicine.* New York: Facts On File, 1995. Young adult book written in a clear, easy-to-understand style on uses of computers and other information technology in science and medicine including telemedicine and space medicine.

Westridge Young Writers' Workshop. *Kids Explore the Gifts of Children with Special Needs.* Santa Fe, N.M.: J. Muir Publishers, 1994. Insightful book for young people about others with handicaps.

Manuel Cardona

PHYSICIST

(1934–)

A highlight of any teacher's life is when his or her former students, now successful themselves, honor their teacher. Professor Manuel Cardona received that life's high point when his career as a solid-state physics researcher and teacher was recognized in a symposium honoring his 60th birthday, which was held in his birthplace, Barcelona, Spain, on September 7, 1994.

Physics is the study of matter and energy and the relation between them. The study of solid-state physics emerged as a separate branch of physics after World War II. It has led to many of the developments in electronics, such as the transistor and microcircuitry, that have revolutionized much of modern audiovisual and information technology.

Leading physicists from around the world, many of them Cardona's former graduate students, gathered at the Universitat Autonoma de Barcelona on his 60th birthday to recognize his outstanding career in physics. They also honored him by reading

Spanish republic, installing dictator Francisco Franco. However, the civil war soon became international in scope and developed into a battleground between Western democracy, fascist Italy, Nazi Germany, and Soviet communism. It also became a proving ground for new weapons of war and afterward was called "a dress rehearsal for World War II."

During the Spanish Civil War many Spaniards were killed or executed, and others lost their homes, businesses, and basic freedoms and were imprisoned. Cardona's father was persecuted merely for being a member of a fraternal organization.

After the war, while attending a state high school in Barcelona, Cardona showed strong interest in both mathematics and physics and decided on a career in science. "I became interested in physics at an early age," said Cardona. "I tinkered with radios, and in high school I liked math class where I had an excellent teacher." He began studying physics at the University of Barcelona in 1950 and received his bachelor's degree *summa cum laude* in 1955.

In 1956 Cardona came to the United States to begin graduate work in physics at Harvard University in Cambridge, Massachusetts. He later returned to Spain to research the effects of light, magnetism, and electricity on germanium and silicon and earned a doctor of science degree from the University of Madrid in 1958.

Germanium and silicon are basic substances that at ordinary temperatures conduct electricity between a metal and an insulator. They both play important parts in the new information technology age of computers and telecommunications. Germanium is a major part of the transistor, and silicon is used to manufacture the silicon chip of the personal computer.

Cardona's use of basic experimental models and investigative tools such as optical spectroscopy has helped to clarify and better identify the properties of these very important elements. Optical spectroscopy involves the study of matter and energy to measure light and vision in which spectra may be photographed to determine the chemical nature of a substance. The research has expanded scientists' knowledge of both semiconductor and superconductor research, providing a foundation on which future developments can be realized in computer and other information technology.

Cardona returned to Harvard, and his further research on non-conducting properties of germanium and silicon led to a doctorate degree in applied science in 1959. That same year Cardona married Inge Hecht, with whom he has three children: Michael, Angela, and Steven.

After receiving his doctorate from Harvard, Cardona joined RCA Laboratories in Switzerland and later in 1959 was transferred to the company's labs in New Jersey.

Both Cardona and his wife became U.S. citizens in 1967. "I became an American citizen partly in order to protest the Vietnam War," said Cardona. The Spanish Civil War and World War II had made him a strong antiwar advocate.

In 1964 Cardona became an associate professor of physics at Brown University in Providence, Rhode Island. Two years later he became a full professor and remained at Brown until 1971 when he accepted the prestigious directorship of the Max Planck Institute of Solid-State Physics in Stuttgart, Germany, where he has remained.

Cardona (left) at a conference in Barcelona, Spain, in 1988 with Pedro Pascual, another noted physicist (Courtesy Max Planck Institute)

Cardona (left) receives accolades from faculty and administrators at Sherbrook University in Canada after delivering the commencement address in 1995. (Courtesy Max Planck Institute)

Cardona's early career in physics not only included spectroscopic analysis of germanium and silicon but also of materials exhibiting superconductivity. Cardona studied such materials from 1962 to 1971. Cardona returned to his study of superconductivity at the Max Planck Institute, but his research has focused on superconductivity at higher temperatures.

Cardona describes his research methods as an attempt to extract the maximum amount of information possible from basic experiments. He is known for his emphasis on simplicity in his research. Many of his over 800 technical papers have become classics in the field and several of his books are used as standard texts at universities. He is also the editor of several technical journals.

In 1989, Cardona began working with Dr. E. E. Haller of the University of California at Berkeley in a program to grow single cell crystals of semiconductors and to investigate their basic physical properties. Their research has yielded a wealth of basic facts that have been added to the study of solid-state physics.

Cardona holds honorary doctorate degrees from universities in several countries. He has been recognized for his research, receiving the 1984 Frank Isakson Prize from the American Physical Society and the 1992 Excellence in Superconductivity Award of the World Congress on Superconductivity.

Cardona has had a great influence in the development of solid-state physics in developing nations, especially in Latin America. Partly for his work as a visiting professor at the University of Buenos Aires in Argentina in 1965, he received an award from the American Physical Society in 1997 for helping encourage the study of physics in Latin America.

"Some of my best work has been done in collaboration with young Latin American physicists, mostly Argentineans, who fled their country as a result of political upheavals or military revolutions," Cardona said.

Cardona recalls one such revolution he witnessed firsthand.

> *M*y Hispanic background has definitely helped me in my work, and it also has enabled me to help other Hispanic scientists from countries where they are or have been persecuted.
>
> —Manuel Cardona

I was teaching in Buenos Aires during the spring of 1966 when the first, if not the bloodiest, of a series of military coups broke out in Argentina. Along with the executions and loss of personal freedoms for many people, the country's budding science programs were severely crippled. Police entered the University of Buenos Aires during what has become known as "the night of the long sticks." They beat up students and faculty members and destroyed the school's computer.

The coup closed the school of physics, and Cardona, who by then was back at Brown University, helped many of the displaced graduate students from the University of Buenos Aires to find new positions at Brown. Many of them since returned to Argentina or went to Brazil and other South American countries where they became professors in science and technology.

Cardona also gave similar help to physics students victimized during political uprisings in Chile in 1969 and another coup in Argentina in 1977. "That Argentina coup led to the 'disappearance' or assassination of a number of physicists I knew," said Cardona. "I was able to save the lives of some of them and also help them find new places to live and work."

Since becoming director of the Max Planck Institute in Stuttgart and besides continuing to conduct research there, Cardona has trained many solid-state physicists. He has helped a number of South American graduate students and visiting scientists from Argentina, Brazil, Mexico, Cuba, and Puerto Rico with their research. He has also worked with physicists from India, China, Korea, and Hong Kong. He participated early in efforts to revive physics after intellectuals lost their teaching positions or were imprisoned during the Cultural Revolution, a period that began in China in 1966 when communist leaders killed or imprisoned intellectuals.

> T*he open dialogue and equal opportunities that democracy guarantees are necessary in the scientific world.*
>
> —Manuel Cardona

"I find physics exciting because my work, mostly in basic science, has been very closely related to the great industrial developments in the field of solid-state engineering which have taken place during my career," said Cardona. "I like to work with people, and my basic scientific work has given me the opportunity to guide bright young men and women and help to get the best out of them. I now believe that is the occupation I am best at."

Chronology

SEPTEMBER 7, 1934	Manuel Cardona is born in Barcelona, Spain
1955	receives bachelor's degree from University of Barcelona
1958	receives master's degree from University of Madria
1959	marries Inge Hecht; receives doctorate degree in applied science from Harvard University; joins staff of RCA Laboratories in Zurich, Switzerland; transferred to RCA Laboratories in Princeton, New Jersey
1964	becomes associate professor of physics at Brown University
1966	becomes professor of physics at Brown
1967	becomes U.S. citizen
1971	becomes director of Max Planck Institute of Solid-State Research in Stuttgart, Germany
1973	becomes honorary professor at University of Stuttgart, Germany
1984	is awarded the Frank Isakson Prize for physics research from the American Physical Society
1987	becomes a member of the National Academy of Sciences of the United States; becomes a visiting professor at the University of California, Berkeley
1989	begins research on basic physical properties of single cell crystals of semiconductors

1992	is honored with the Excellence in Superconductivity Award of the World Conference on Superconductivity
1994	receives honorary doctorates from Sherbrooke University, Canada, and University of Regensburg, Germany; is honored with symposium on solid-state physics at Universitat Autonoma de Barcelona, Spain
1995	receives honorary doctorate from University of Rome, Italy

Further Reading

Book about Manuel Cardona

McMurray, Emily J. *Notable Twentieth-Century Scientists.* Detroit: Gale, 1995. Brief biography of Cardona.

Books on Related Topics

Feynman, Richard Phillips. *Six Easy Pieces: Essentials of Physics.* Reading, Mass.: Helix Books, 1995. Basic principles of physics explained for young adults.

Freeman, Ira Maximillian. *Physics Made Simple.* New York: Doubleday, 1990. Young readers needing a basic understanding of physics should be able to get it here.

Kerrod, Robin. *The Simon & Schuster Reader's Guide Book of Science.* New York: Simon & Schuster, 1991. Illustrated, simplified explanations of basics of science including physics.

Pedro Sánchez

SOIL SCIENTIST
(1940–)

When Cuban-born Pedro Sánchez was studying soil management at Cornell University in Ithaca, New York, in 1964, he read about the ancient method of "slash-and-burn" farming. People were still using this method in some places. They would cut down trees in forested areas with machetes, then dry and burn them. The remaining ash would fertilize one or two crops, but then the land would lose its nutrients, so the farmers would have to migrate and would do the same in another part of the forest. Soil conservationists considered it an unproductive farming method and cautioned that when carried out in rain forests, it also contributed to tropical deforestation, a major cause of global warming.

Sánchez believed there had to be a better way to farm. In 1971, while an assistant professor of soil management at North Carolina State University at Raleigh, North Carolina, he was given an opportunity to find that better way. The university had a long history of studying soil conditions in various parts of the world, and Sánchez

Pedro Sánchez is a leading soil scientist who specializes in research to overcome tropical deforestation while finding ways to improve and preserve management of tropical soils for sustained food production. (Courtesy International Centre for Research in Agroforestry)

was assigned to head a soil management project at Yurimaguas in the jungles of Peru.

Working conditions were crude. A gas generator was hooked up with barbed wire to jump-start a drier so that Sánchez and his helpers could dry plant tissue. The samples were then ground in order to analyze them. The only communication with Peru's capital city of Lima for advice and support was via a shortwave radio that a local land owner let Sánchez use each Friday afternoon.

Political conditions were worse. In 1972, Peru's military took over the government. Sánchez lost his office and moved it to the International Potato Center, also in Lima. A year later, just as research began to go well there, the Peruvian air force threatened to build an air strip through the research station, exactly where Sánchez's helpers had neatly cleared the land and smoothed it for rice farming.

"By luck, the air force minister heard an interview I had given in Spanish over Voice of America about the Yurimaguas project," Sánchez said. "He realized how important it was to agricultural development in that area and ordered the airport be put somewhere else."

Yet another threat to the project in the early 1970s came from a far-left Peruvian political group called "People Without Bosses." The group stormed into the research station's office and threatened to "rid the area of gringo [American or foreign] influence." Sánchez, forewarned that they were coming, was waiting there for them, casually puffing one of the cigars he was seldom without.

When the leaders of the angry group demanded to know who he was, Sánchez waved his cigar with a flourish and replied in Spanish, "I'm from Cuba. I'm here to help the farmers."

Hearing that, the group was all smiles. "They left with the impression that we were a program of the Cuban government," Sánchez recalled. "I didn't try to correct that impression, and neither did the people of Yurimaguas. They liked us, gringos or not."

Sánchez's years at the jungle research station in Peru became the highlights of a career that has been devoted to improving soil and crop management for a world growing rapidly in population and in need of more productive and healthier food sources.

☆ ☆ ☆

Pedro Antonio Sánchez was born October 7, 1940, in Havana, Cuba, the oldest of four children of Pedro Antonio Sánchez and Georgina San Martín Sánchez. His parents owned a farm and fertilizer business, and he became interested in soil science at an early age, traveling throughout Cuba with his father. His mother was a high school teacher and pharmacist.

After graduating from the high school at the Colegio de la Salle in Havana in 1958, Sánchez emigrated. He went to the United States and enrolled at Cornell University because not only was it a leader in the study of soil science but both his parents had graduated from that university.

Sánchez intended to complete his education abroad and then return to Cuba to help in the family businesses, but political events forced a change in his plan. During his sophomore year at Cornell, in 1960, his parents' farm and fertilizer business were confiscated by Cuban president Fidel Castro's communist regime, which forbade private business ownership. The Sánchez family had lost everything,

> *I'm a soil scientist because ever since I was a boy, I've loved the earth. I'm still a kid, because I like to play with dirt.*
>
> —Pedro Sánchez

so they fled to Miami where they started a new life. Sánchez decided to remain in the United States, and that same year he became a U.S. citizen.

In 1962, Sánchez received his bachelor of science degree in agronomy, the science of soil management and the production of field crops. Two years later he received his master's degree in soil science from Cornell.

Sánchez married a fellow student, Wendy Levin, in 1965, and they later had three children: Jennifer, Evan, and Juliana. That same year he also began doctorate studies at Cornell. From 1965 to 1968 he worked as a graduate assistant in soil science in the University of the Philippines–Cornell Graduate Education program in Los Baños, Philippines. He conducted research for his doctorate and also taught soil fertility courses.

After receiving his doctorate degree in soil science from Cornell in 1968, Sánchez became an assistant professor of soil science at North Carolina State University (NCSU) at Raleigh, North Carolina. He quickly became involved in the university's soil conservation program in South America. From 1968 to 1971 he was coleader of the university's National Rice Program of Peru, an agricultural mission established jointly by NCSU and Peru's Ministry of Agriculture and the Universidad Nacional Pedro Ruíz Gallo of Peru. From the program's base in Lima, Sánchez supervised a nationwide soil management research program with a staff of 60 technicians whose primary objective was to help Peruvian farmers improve and increase their rice production.

It was in 1971, after a harrowing prop-plane flight across the Andes mountains that Sánchez, accompanied by Stanley Buol, also a professor of soil science, first set eyes on the little town of Yurimaguas in the jungles of Peru. They had flown there to begin conducting soil and rice management field research in the area. Little did Sánchez know that the project would continue there through military coups, financial crises, and the threat of terrorism for the next 20 years.

Yurimaguas is a remote town of about 20,000 inhabitants in the state of Loreto, just slightly south of the equator, by the Huallaga River; it is the last major river-boat port upstream from the Amazon. The town was named after two local forest tribes, the Yuris and the Omaguas.

Shortly after their arrival at the dirt landing strip at Yurimaguas, Sánchez and Buol set out to visit some Peruvian experiments with rice. Along the way, Sánchez advised his superior to take off his boots before crossing the shallow but swift-running river. Sánchez had learned earlier that a worker had worn his boots into the river, where they filled with water and dragged him into the current; he drowned. Buol appreciated Sánchez's warning and said to others watching, "I think I can work with this guy."

The pair spent two weeks in the jungle, scouting sites for rice crop research, then returned to Yurimaguas where they found the farmers willing to cooperate and the acidity of the soil sufficiently elevated for their study. Perhaps more important, a local rancher, Domingo Loero, had donated a large tract of his land to the government of Peru for agricultural research.

With a team of Peruvian scientists, Sánchez and Buol tramped Loero's land for days, through worn-out pastures, dense scrub, and heavy jungle, studying the soil and marking the limits of their new research station on aerial photographs.

In a retrospective article about NCSU's management project in Peru over 20 years, written by Neil Caudle for the university's magazine, Sánchez reminisced on the experience. Explaining why an American university would want to conduct soil research in a South American jungle, Sánchez said "Most of the reasons are practical. . . . There were grants to be had, myths to be debunked, scientific curiosity to be satisfied, students to train, careers to advance. And there were precedents, too. NCSU was no stranger to the tropics. We had been learning a lot about tropical soils in the savannas of Brazil. And we had been in Peru years earlier, in 1952, conducting agricultural research projects on the coast and in the mountains."

Sánchez also echoed the words of Charles McCants who became head of NCSU's Soil Science Department just weeks after the first grant to work in Yurimaguas came through: "Some of us also felt a sense of responsibility. We believed that people who are privileged with education and material resources have a responsibility to help people who are less fortunate. We had seen what it could mean to people to make farms more productive. We wanted to give people in the tropics an alternative to the poverty of poorly managed soil and agriculture."

Sánchez's colleagues say he tapped all of these motives with his energy, enthusiasm, and idealism strongly rooted in reality. But progress was slow. Dale Bandy, who was from Ohio and joined the Yurimaguas project five years later, recalled his first impression of the research station:

> You came down this cow path to a creek, and then you had to park your car and wade the creek and walk the next two or three kilometers out to the research station. They called it a "research station," but it was just one pitiful little bamboo hut and a patch cleared out of the jungle. I was amazed at how much research had already come out of that place.

Sánchez found an able assistant in Bandy and over the next few years the research station expanded with laboratories, offices, and a lunchroom. As Sánchez's research from the Yurimaguas project was published in journals, scientists from all over the world came there to study and add their knowledge of soil management by holding meetings and workshops.

"When we started at Yurimaguas, we had no idea we would be there twenty years," said Sánchez. "Long-term research is totally against most funding patterns. But if your goal is sustainable agriculture, having that long-term data is absolutely essential." Sustainable agriculture is a system based on the wise use of renewable natural resources for the common good of the area over time.

Sánchez says the soil management work at Yurimaguas has resulted in several important findings: "We have destroyed the myth that Amazonian soils are useless [because they are not rich enough to plant food crops such as corn or beans.] We have changed the world's opinion of these soils. The project has proved the benefits of sustainable agriculture and that the Amazonian soils can be farmed continuously, in a manner that is economically and ecologically sound. That's the importance of the Yurimaguas program."

Sánchez continued his work in South America from 1971 to 1983, first becoming leader of the Tropical Soils Program responsible for field soil research projects in the Cerrado of Brazil, along the Amazon of Peru, and in Central America. Then he became coordinator for the Beef–Tropical Pastures Program, Centro Internacional de Agricultura Tropical in Cali, Colombia, supervising activities of about 40 scientists throughout tropical Latin America. From 1982 to 1983, Sánchez became chief of NCSU's soil conservation mission to Lima, Peru, supervising the development of the country's agricultural research and education system.

Meanwhile, Sánchez had become associate professor of soil science at NCSU in 1973, and six years later, a full professor. His Hispanic background and ability to speak English, Spanish, and Portuguese enabled him to gain the confidence and support of Latin Americans with whom he worked.

Sánchez in West Sumatra, Indonesia, in 1992, on one of his frequent field trips studying soil management in forests and jungles around the world (Courtesy International Centre for Research in Agroforestry)

In 1984 Sánchez began expanding his soil conservation work into other parts of the world. For the next seven years he was coordinator of the Tropical Soils Program at NCSU, supervising soil management projects throughout Bolivia, Indonesia, and Madagascar. From 1990 to 1991, he was also director of the Center for World Environment and Sustainable Development, a joint project sponsored by NCSU, the University of North Carolina at Chapel Hill, and Duke University.

Sánchez and his wife had divorced in 1989, and the following year he married Cheryl Palm, a soil scientist with whom he worked at Yurimaguas. Then in 1991 Sánchez made a major change in his life after becoming professor emeritus of soil science and forestry at NCSU: He left South America to accept a new challenge in Africa by becoming director general of the International Centre for Research in Agroforestry (ICRAF) at Nairobi, Kenya. Agroforestry is an ecologically based, natural resources management system that, through the integration of trees in farms and in the agricultural landscape, diversifies and sustains production for increased social, economic, and environmental benefits for land users at all levels.

> S*cience can be a lot of fun, and I've always liked big challenges. Soil management provides an exciting challenge to find ways to feed the hungry world.*
>
> —Pedro Sánchez

When Sánchez joined ICRAF it was an international council. Under his leadership, it has become an international research center with a global program in agroforestry, working in six tropical ecoregions.

Sánchez's wife joined him in Nairobi and has helped him both in his work and also in writing on soil science. One of his books, *Properties and Management of Soils of the Tropics,* is among the top 10 best-selling books in soil science worldwide.

Sánchez is a member of the American Society of Agronomy, the Soil Science Society of America, and the Asociación Latinoamericana de Cien-

Sánchez says he is a farmer who also loves to fish. When not working as a soil scientist he is in pursuit of marlin, as he was in 1990, fishing off the Guanacaste coast in Costa Rica. (Courtesy International Centre for Research in Agroforestry)

cias Agrícolas. He is also a member of the International Soil Science Society and chairs its Soil Fertility and Plant Nutrition Commission.

In recognition of his work in soil management, Sánchez has received decorations from the governments of Colombia and Peru. In 1979, he received the Diploma de Honor from the Instituto Colombiano Agropecuario. In 1984, the Peruvian government awarded him the Orden de Mérito Agrícola, an honor seldom given to a non-Peruvian citizen.

Sánchez continues his work in soil management in Kenya. He said it is a thrill when farmers tell him they are excited about the big, healthy ears of corn they grow because of his agricultural advice.

Despite his love of farming and the land, his main hobby is deep-sea fishing. He has caught a 365-pound shark and several 100-pound marlin but let them go. "A dream of my life," Sánchez said, "is to land a really big, 400-pound marlin. I know I'm a farmer, but only then can I call myself a fisherman."

PEDRO SÁNCHEZ

Chronology

OCTOBER 7, 1940	Pedro Antonio Sánchez is born in Havana, Cuba
1958	immigrates to United States
1960	becomes U.S. citizen
1962	receives bachelor degree in agronomy from Cornell University
1964	receives master's degree in soil science from Cornell University
1965	marries Wendy Levin
1965–68	works as graduate assistant in soil science in the Philippines
1968	receives doctorate degree in soil science from Cornell University; becomes assistant professor in soil science at North Carolina State University (NCSU)
1968–71	serves as coleader of NCSU's National Rice Program of Peru
1971–76	serves as leader of NCSU's Tropical Soils Program in Brazil and Peru
1973	becomes associate professor of soil science at NCSU
1977–79	serves as coordinator of Beef–Tropical Pastures Program in Cali, Colombia
1979	becomes professor of soil science at NCSU
1979–82	serves as coordinator of Tropical Soils Program at NCSU
1982–83	serves as chief of NCSU Mission to Peru

1984–91	serves as coordinator of NCSU's Tropical Soils Program in Peru, Bolivia, Indonesia, and Madagascar
1989	is divorced from Wendy Levin
1990	marries Cheryl Palm
1990–1991	serves as director of Center for World Environment and Sustainable Development
1991 TO PRESENT	becomes professor emeritus of soil science and forestry at NCSU and director general of International Centre for Research in Agroforestry, Kenya

Further Reading

Book about Pedro Sánchez
McMurray, Emily J. *Notable Twentieth-Century Scientists.* Detroit: Gale, 1995. Brief biography of Sánchez.

Books on Related Topics
Aldis, Rodney. *Rainforests.* New York: Dillon Press, 1991. Interesting study of rainforests and efforts to preserve them. Well written for young readers.

Carson, Rachel. *Silent Spring.* Boston: Houghton-Mifflin, 1987. Orginally published in 1962, this reprint is a highly recommended analysis of how misuse of natural resources affects the health of all life on the planet.

Cherrington, Mark. *Degradation of the Land.* New York: Chelsea House, 1992. Good study for young readers about the problem of land misuse and how soil conservation can help solve it.

Dunphy, Madeleine. *Here is the Tropical Rainforest.* New York: Hyperion, 1994. A good overview of rainforests and their use and misuse, for young readers.

Greene, Carol. *Caring for Our Land.* Hillside, N.J.: Enslow, 1991. Good young adult book on wise use of the land.

Herda, D. J., and Margaret L. Madden. *Land Use and Abuse.* New York: Watts, 1990. Good, easy-to-read, basic young adult book on soil conservation and preservation of forests and wetlands.

Mario Molina

ENVIRONMENTAL CHEMIST
(1943–)

While teaching chemistry in 1995 at the Massachusetts Institute of Technology in Cambridge, Mexican-born Professor Mario Molina received a telephone call from a colleague in Stockholm, Sweden, who was a member of that country's prestigious Royal Academy of Sciences. Molina learned that the academy had just named him a winner of the Nobel Prize for chemistry.

"It was the most unexpected and exciting thing that ever happened to me," Molina recalled later. "I had been living a quiet life teaching chemistry and doing research on the impact chemicals have on the environment. Suddenly, my name was in newspapers and on television, and a few months later I went to Stockholm to received the award."

The Nobel Prize came as a surprise to Molina, but others in his profession knew he deserved the honor. It brought him recognition for years of research into chemical causes of pollution that affect our lives in many ways.

Mario Molina, an environmental chemist, won the Nobel Prize in chemistry in 1995 for research on the impact of humanmade chemicals on the environment and in particular on ozone pollution. (Courtesy Massachusetts Institute of Technology)

Mario José Molina was born on March 19, 1943, in Mexico City to Roberto Molina and Leonor Molina-Pasquel. His father was a lawyer in private practice who also taught at the National Autonomous University of Mexico and later became Mexico's ambassador to Ethiopia, Australia, and the Philippines.

Molina first became interested in science when he was a boy. "I started playing with a chemistry set and a toy microscope," he recalled years later.

> I remember one of my first experiments. I placed some lettuce in water and let it rot for a few days. I then placed a drop of the stinky water under the microscope.
>
> Few experiences in life compare with that magic moment! The rotten lettuce was teeming with life, and I was able to observe with my own eyes what those famous scientists had discovered so many years earlier. I have been hooked on science since that time.

Molina then converted the family's bathroom into a laboratory and spent hours playing with chemistry sets. He also read biographies of famous scientists and learned about what he later called "a mysterious and marvelous world that appeared totally inaccessible to me at that time."

While attending elementary school in Mexico City, Molina learned to play the violin. It made him consider pursuing a career in music, but by the time he was 11, he decided to become a research chemist.

Throughout high school in Mexico City, Molina's friends thought science was something for school but not, as he did, for play or enjoyment. After graduating from high school in 1960, Molina enrolled in the chemical engineering program at the Universidad Nacional Autónoma de México. "I discovered a new dimension to my involvement with science—interaction with my fellow students and teachers," Molina recalled.

communicate the CFC-ozone issue not only to other scientists but also to policymakers and to the news media. We realized this was the only way to insure that society would take some measures to alleviate the problem."

Molina and Rowland were invited to testify before the U.S. House of Representatives's Subcommittee on Public Health and Environment in 1974. Their testimony led to worldwide concern about ozone pollution, and manufacturers were instructed to begin searching for alternative gases for their products.

Molina refined his studies and, together with Rowland, published more data on CFCs and the destruction of the ozone layer. Their articles appeared in 1974 in the *Journal of Physical Chemistry* and *Geophysical Research Letter,* and a detailed study entitled "The Ozone Question" was published in *Science* magazine.

In 1975 Molina was appointed to the faculty at the University of California at Irvine as an assistant professor. Two years later, after the birth of their son, Felipe, Molina's wife joined his research group. "Throughout the years, she has been very supportive and understanding of my preoccupation with work and the intense nature of my research," Molina said.

After seven years at Irvine and having become an associate professor in 1979, Molina decided in 1982 to move to a nonacademic position. He became a member of the Molecular Physics and Chemistry Section of the Jet Propulsion Laboratory at California Institute of Technology (CalTech) at Pasadena. He was named senior research scientist two years later and held the position for another five years, conducting measurements and developing techniques for the study of newly emerging chemistry problems.

Molina and Rowland's research laid the groundwork for the discovery in 1985 that massive decreases of ozone had occurred over Antarctica, resulting in a "hole" in the ozone. They found that the chemicals most directly linked to the phenomenon were CFCs. Their study led to the 1987 United Nations's Montreal Protocol on Substances That Deplete the Ozone Layer, an international treaty in which 93 nations, including the United States, agreed to ban the production of CFCs from 1996 on.

Molina left CalTech in 1989 to become a professor of atmospheric chemistry in the department of earth, atmospheric, and planetary sciences at the Massachusetts Institute of Technology (MIT) and also a professor in MIT's department of chemistry. Since then he and his research group, which still includes his wife, have continued studying global atmospheric chemistry issues.

Molina shared the 1995 Nobel Prize in chemistry with his longtime colleague, Professor Rowland, and with Professor Paul Crutzen. The honor was for their work in atmospheric chemistry, particularly concerning the formation and decomposition of ozone and their theory that chlorofluorocarbons produced by industry deplete the ozone layer of the stratosphere. It was the first time the Nobel Prize recognized research into human-made impacts of the environment.

Molina has published more than 50 scientific papers, most of them dealing with his work on the ozone layer and the chemistry of the atmosphere. He was elected to the National Academy of Sciences in 1993, and the following year he was named by President Bill Clinton to serve on the 18-member President's Committee of Advisors on Science and Technology.

Molina and his wife live in Lexington, Massachusetts. Their son, Felipe, is a student at Brown University in Providence, Rhode Island, studying science.

Although he no longer spends much time in the laboratory, having made the switch back to teaching, Molina says,

> *I am heartened and humbled that I was able to do something that not only contributed to our understanding of atmospheric chemistry, but also had a profound impact on the global environment.*
>
> —Mario Molina

I very much enjoy working with my graduate and postdoctoral students, who provide me with invaluable intellectual stimulus.

MARIO MOLINA

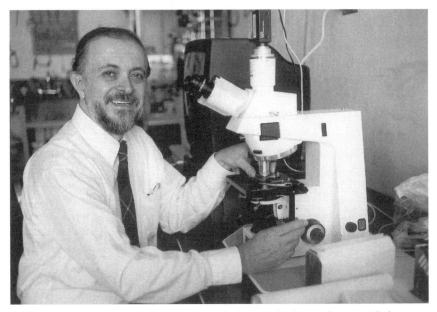

When Molina is not in his laboratory using the latest technology in his research, he travels giving talks about new developments in the atmospheric sciences. (Courtesy Massachusetts Institute of Technology)

I also have benefited from teaching. As I try to explain my views to students with critical and open minds, I find myself continually being challenged to go back and rethink ideas. I now see teaching and research as complementary, mutually reinforcing activities.

When I first chose the project to investigate the fate of chlorofluorocarbons in the atmosphere, it was simply out of scientific curiosity. I did not consider at that time the environmental consequences of what Sherry and I had set out to study. "Sherry" Rowland has always been a wonderful mentor and colleague. I cherish my years of association with him and my friendship with him and his wife Joan.

Molina said that being Hispanic American had little if any impact on his career. "One of the very rewarding aspects of my work has been the interaction with a superb group of colleagues and friends in the atmospheric sciences community," he said.

Molina frequently lectures to minority students, to encourage them to pursue careers in science. "Find some area of study you like, something that you can really become interested in," he tells young people. "Then remain focused and try to excel in your work of choice. Be vitally interested and committed to your work. Try to work in teams and share your knowledge. Above all, don't forget that learning and discovering are extremely enjoyable. Of course, you need patience and perseverance, but in the end, your studies will give you a very rewarding experience."

Chronology

MARCH 19, 1943	Mario José Molina is born in Mexico City
1965	graduates from the Universidad Nacional Autónoma de México with degree in chemical engineering
1967	graduates from University of Freiberg, West Germany, with master's degree in chemistry
1968	immigrates to United States and enrolls at University of California at Berkeley
1972	receives doctorate from University of California at Berkeley
1973	marries Luisa Y. Tan; begins postdoctoral studies in physical chemistry at University of California at Irvine
1975	becomes assistant professor of chemistry at University of California, Irvine
1979	becomes associate professor at University of California–Irvine

1982	becomes member of technical staff at Jet Propulsion Laboratory at California Institute of Technology
1984	is named senior research scientist at Jet Propulsion Laboratory
1989	becomes both professor of atmospheric chemistry at Massachusettes Institute of Technology's department of earth, atmosphere, and planetary sciences, and professor in department of chemistry
1994	is named to the President's Committee of Advisors on Science and Technology by President Bill Clinton
1995	shares Nobel Prize in chemistry with F. Sherwood Rowland and Paul Crutzen
1996 TO PRESENT	continues chemistry professorship at MIT and research on ozone and other chemical impacts on the environment

Further Reading

Book by Mario Molina
Molina, Mario. *The Science of Global Change: The Impact of Human Activities on the Environment.* Monograph (with Luisa Molina) "Stratospheric Ozone." Washington, D.C.: American Chemical Society, 1992. Adult scientific book that may be difficult reading for young adults.

Book about Mario Molina
McMurray, Emily J. *Notable Twentieth-Century Scientists.* Detroit: Gale, 1995. For adult readers but includes a brief, relatively unscientific biography of Molina.

Books on Related Topics

Dolan, Edward F. *Our Poisoned Sky*. New York: Cobblehill/Dutton, 1991. Good, basic young adult report on air pollution and damage to the ozone layer.

Duden, Jane. *The Ozone Layer*. New York: Crestwood House, 1990. Young adult book about ozone's benefits and dangers.

Greene, Carol. *Caring for Our Air*. Hillside, N.J.: Enslow, 1991. Easy reading about wise environmental programs that keep our air clean and safe.

Johnson, Rebecca L. *Investigating the Ozone Hole*. Minneapolis: Lerner, 1993. A good reference book for young readers on dangers of ozone pollution in the atmosphere.

Miller, Christina G., and Louise A. Berry. *Air Alert—Rescuing the Earth's Atmosphere*. New York: Atheneum, 1996. Young readers learn about efforts to keep the air we breathe from becoming polluted.

Nardo, Don. *Ozone*. San Diego: Lucent, 1991. A young person's basic book about ozone and its influence on the environment.

Henry Díaz

METEOROLOGIST
(1948–)

" If you've never been in a hurricane off the ocean, you can't imagine the force of the wind, or the raging waters that can cause great destruction and take hundreds of lives," said Henry Díaz, a leading authority on violent weather.

As a boy born and raised in Cuba in the 1950s, Díaz had seen several of the century's most devastating hurricanes ravage his native land. The island nation in the Caribbean just south of Florida is in what is called the "Hurricane Belt," subject to wind storms that churn the ocean into walls of floodwater that sweep over everything in their path. Later, as a teenager living in Miami, Díaz saw the destruction caused when the area was hit by two of the most violent hurricanes of the century.

"For as long as I can remember, because of those experiences, I have been excited by violent weather," Díaz said in an interview. It is what led him to become a meteorologist, a scientist who studies the atmosphere and weather.

Henry Díaz, a meteorologist, is an atmospheric scientist and one of the leading researchers of the devastating El Niño weather phenomenon. (Courtesy National Oceanic and Atmospheric Administration)

Díaz has become one of the world's leading authorities on El Niño, a devastating warm weather phenomenon occurring periodically off the coast of South America that has created some of the most damaging rainstorms and droughts around the world over hundreds of years.

☆ ☆ ☆

Henry Frank Díaz, son of Francisco Díaz, an attorney of Spanish and French descent, and María Vías Díaz of Spanish-Catalan descent, was born in Santiago de Cuba on July 15, 1948. Cuba, the largest island in the Caribbean Sea, is located about 90 miles south of the United States, across the Straits of Florida.

When Díaz was a boy in the 1940s, Cuba was a democracy governed by various presidents. This lasted until 1952 when Fulgencio Batista, a former president, imposed authoritarian rule. His leadership as president failed to improve conditions for a country long mired in poverty and political upheaval.

Dissent began to grow among the Cuban people and the army during Batista's presidency. One of his opponents, a lawyer named Fidel Castro, organized a guerrilla movement in 1956 that resulted in the Cuban Revolution. Batista fled to Spain in 1959.

Castro became dictator in Cuba, instituting reforms but challenging U.S. economic and political interests there. Cuba became the only communist-allied state in the Americas, with close economic and military ties to the Soviet Union. Díaz's father and many other Cubans did not approve of Castro's radical communist government, and about a million people left the country after 1959, most of them settling in the United States.

Díaz was 11 years old in 1959, and he and his parents moved to Havana, Cuba's capital on the north coast about 100 miles south of Key West, Florida. Since Cuba is in the path of sometimes very violent weather, especially hurricanes, Díaz became interested in tropical weather. "I became excited by the passage of tropical squalls," he said in an interview. "I secretly hoped that one of the many hurricanes which occasionally threatened the island during the late summer months and autumn might pass right over Havana."

Díaz's father had become politically active against Castro, so it became unsafe for the family to live in Cuba any longer. When he was thirteen, Díaz's parents sent him to live with relatives in the United States, but they remained in Havana. He lived with an uncle in New Jersey for four years, until his parents and sister immigrated to Miami, and he joined them there.

In October 1963, Hurricane Flora swept over the island of Haiti in the Caribbean and killed 4,000 people. Díaz and tens of thousands of others on mainland America watched the violent skies to the south and feared Flora would turn in their direction. Instead, the storm struck Cuba and then wore itself out over the ocean.

The following year, when Díaz was 16 and attending high school in Miami, Hurricane Cleo headed toward the city. "The skies to the southeast of Miami looked blacker and more stormy than I'd ever seen them," said Díaz. Cleo slammed into Haiti, barely recovering from Hurricane Flora the year before, then began to turn toward the southern Florida coast.

"As Cleo came closer to Miami, my family and I were living in an apartment building," Díaz recalled. "The walls were shaking and we heard the roar of the winds. We thought our windows would be blown out, but we were lucky and there was just minor damage. All around the city, though, there was a lot of destruction. Roofs and outer walls of buildings were ripped off. Power lines blew down and burst into flaming colors, setting off explosions like fireworks. We were without electricity for several days. Everywhere in Miami, there was a lot of wreckage."

After a week of ravaging the United States, Hurricane Cleo dwindled off the Georgia coast. The storm caused more than $500 million damage in Miami and elsewhere along the eastern coast. Some 200 people were injured, but miraculously, no one was killed.

After graduating from high school in Miami in 1967, Díaz attended Florida State University in Tallahassee. He met Marla Cremin, also a college student, at a dance, and they were married two years later. He became a U.S. citizen in 1970 and a year later graduated from Florida State University with a bachelor of science degree in meteorology.

Meteorologists observe weather conditions around the world and try to understand what causes their development and predict what the weather is going to do next. To accomplish this

It was during violent storms when I was a teenager that I decided to make the study of weather and storms such as hurricanes my life's work.

—Henry Díaz

involves an understanding of chemistry, physics, mathematics, geology, oceanography, and other sciences. Meteorologists work with computers, radar, satellites, barometers, and other instruments to measure temperature, air pressure, humidity, and wind speed.

"After getting my bachelor's degree, I still had a strong interest in tropical weather and climate, so I decided to continue pursuing my education in the same field," Díaz said. He received a master of science degree in atmospheric science from the University of Miami in 1974. A son, Christopher, was born to Díaz and his wife the following year.

After getting his master's degree, Díaz began a career with the National Oceanic and Atmospheric Administration (NOAA), part of the U.S. Department of Commerce. He was assigned as a meteorologist in NOAA's Environmental Data Service in Washington, D.C.

After a year, Díaz moved with his wife and son to Asheville, North Carolina, where he worked for the Climate Analysis Division of NOAA's National Climatic Data Center. "It was there that I became involved professionally in the study of climatic variability and change," Díaz said.

In 1980, after the birth of a daughter, Susana, Díaz moved his family to Boulder, Colorado, where he was transferred to NOAA's Climate Research Program, part of the administration's Environmental Sciences Group. Four years later, he became acting director of the program.

Meanwhile, Díaz continued his academic studies at the University of Colorado at Boulder on an NOAA scholarship. He received his doctorate in 1985 from the Department of Geography with a specialization in climatology.

Díaz has worked for various units of NOAA's Environmental Research Laboratories in Boulder for most of his professional career, on a variety of climate research and climate impact issues. From 1986 to 1989 he worked for the climatic research division of NOAA's Air Resources Laboratory. From 1989 to 1993 he worked in NOAA's Climate Monitoring and Diagnostics Laboratory.

Díaz studies atmospheric circulation maps to chart the course of tornadoes, hurricanes, and other violent weather. (Courtesy National Oceanic and Atmospheric Administration)

In 1992, Díaz wrote a book, *El Niño: Historical and Paleoclimatic Aspects of the Southern Oscillation,* which was published by Cambridge University Press in England.

In 1993, Díaz became a research climatologist in the Climate Diagnostics Center of NOAA's Environmental Research Laboratories in Boulder. He has focused on the impact of climatic variation on water resources of the western United States.

Díaz has authored or coauthored more than 50 articles and reports for scientific journals about the nature of climatic fluctuations both regional and global, from periods of a year to a century. He is a fellow of the Cooperative Institute for Research in Environmental Sciences of the University of Colorado at Boulder and an adjunct associate professor, teaching geography.

Díaz also is an expert on the El Niño/Southern Oscillation (ENSO) weather phenomenon, which has become his main scientific interest. The name El Niño is Spanish for "the boy child" or "the infant." The reference is to the Christ child, since just about every year, beginning near Christmas, a weak warm current appears off the coasts of Peru and Ecuador. The term was originally used by Peruvian fishermen in the 19th century to refer to a Christmas-time warming of coastal sea surface temperature that killed many fish in the area.

Today, weather researchers know that El Niño starts in the tropical South Pacific. Every few years, giant regions of high- and low-pressure air along the equator over the South Pacific suddenly switch places. This seemingly harmless shift sets off a meteorological chain reaction that sends often devastating climate shock waves around the globe.

In the 1960s, various El Niños were blamed for abnormally high sea surface temperatures and heavy rains in Peru's and Ecuador's usually very dry coastal plains. Heavy rains during El Niño also occurred in the usually dry zones of the Canton Island and Christmas Islands region along the Pacific equator. At the same time, other islands in the Pacific got no rain and experienced drier than normal conditions. El Niño events have also resulted in droughts that have caused crop failures and famines in various parts of the world.

Díaz made a special study of the highly destructive El Niño that occurred during the winter of 1982–83. Considered to be the strongest El Niño of the century, it caused great damage and suffering in many parts of the world including the United States. Its effects of too much or too little rain extended far out into the Pacific and nearly a quarter of the way around the globe from Peru and Ecuador.

In normally sunny California, El Niño came out of the Pacific Ocean in January 1983 and brought nine days of strong winds and torrential rains. Dropping as much as 16 inches of rain on Los Angeles, San Francisco, and just about every town in between, they created floods, mudslides, and record high tides. Californians thought the Pacific climate, generally mild, had gone crazy. The rains caused more than $1.3 billion in property damage, killed 12 people, and forced 10,000 Californians to leave their homes.

Wet winter weather resulted all across the southern United States and Cuba, lasting well through the spring. Flooding and mudslides from melting heavy snows battered Utah. Waves of mud and debris poured down from canyons, forcing hundreds to leave their homes.

On a worldwide scale, the El Niño of 1982–83 caused $8.11 billion of flood, hurricane, rain, drought, and fire damage and destruction across five continents. Besides hundreds of lives lost, it spawned a rash of cyclones that left thousands more people homeless.

Díaz points to expected El Niño impacts on U.S. weather for the next season. (Courtesy National Oceanic and Atmospheric Administration)

Díaz and other scientists came to agree that a major warming event such as El Niño directly affects weather over at least a third of the world and perhaps over as much as half. Long a mystery, El Niño is now believed to be the largest single weather influence on the planet.

It is this weather phenomenon that has prompted Díaz to join a select group of meteorological colleagues in trying to understand better. One major goal is to be able to develop methods for making weather predictions beyond one season, at least for certain areas during El Niño conditions. They have important work to do because some computer weather experts predict that El Niños will become more severe and more frequent over the next century.

As this book was being written, the El Niño of 1997–98 was creating havoc across the globe, bringing heavy and damaging rains to some parts of the world and drought to others. In the Philippines and throughout Southeast Asia, much-needed rain did not come, and the area suffered its worst drought in 50 years. Dry conditions created fires that destroyed 1.9 million acres of forest and left 20 million people sick and near starvation. El Niño was blamed for $1.4 billion in lost timber, lost tourism, and increased health costs in Southeast Asia alone.

Díaz was among the scientists who were kept extra busy monitoring the effects of the 1997–98 El Niño. "Hopefully," said Díaz, "our research of this latest El Niño can help us predict when future El Niños will develop and give potential victims around the world a chance to prepare for them."

Díaz likes his work very much, but he likes to relax, too. In his spare time he enjoys gardening, hiking, camping, cross-country skiing, and listening to music. "Although I thoroughly enjoy Colorado's superb mountain scenery, pine-scented air, and beautiful sunsets," Díaz said, "I also try to get away to the beach as often as I can, which is not enough."

Díaz's wife teaches at an elementary school in Boulder and also is an educational consultant. Their son, Christopher, is in college studying business and finance, and their daughter, Susana, is attending high school.

Díaz said that his Cuban birth and Hispanic background were not significant issues in his career. Díaz encourages young people to take an interest in meteorology or any other subject that interests them. "Follow your bliss," he encourages, "as the philosopher Joseph Campbell has said. If given choices, go with what excites you rather than what might pay the best. Set goals and go after them."

Chronology

JULY 15, 1948	Henry Frank Díaz is born in Santiago de Cuba
1959	moves with family to Havana, Cuba's capital
1962	immigrates to United States
1964	is reunited with family in Miami
1967	graduates from high school in Miami; enrolls at Florida State University
1969	marries Marla Cremin
1970	becomes U.S. citizen
1971	graduates from Florida State with bachelor's degree in meteorology
1974	graduates from University of Miami with master of science degree in atmospheric science; starts lifelong career with National Oceanic and Atmospheric Administration (NOAA)
1984	becomes acting director of NOAA's Climate Research Program in Boulder, Colorado
1985	receives doctorate from geography department of the University of Colorado at Boulder

1986–89	works for Climatic Research Division of NOAA's Air Resources Laboratory
1989–93	works in NOAA's Climate Monitoring and Diagnostics Laboratory
1992	publishes study of *El Niño*
1993–PRESENT	works as research climatologist in Climate Diagnostics Center of NOAA's Environmental Research Laboratories in Boulder

Further Reading

Book by Henry Díaz

Díaz, Henry. *El Niño: Historical and Paleoclimatic Aspects of the Southern Oscillation.* Coauthored by V. Markgraf. Cambridge, England: Cambridge University Press, 1992. An extensive study of the El Niño weather phenomenon. Scientific reading intended for adults.

Books and Information about Henry Díaz

National Oceanic & Atmospheric Administration. "Biographical Data—Henry Díaz." Boulder, Colo.: National Oceanic & Atmospheric Administration, 1997. Short, easy-to-read biographical material on Díaz.

McMurray, Emily J. *Notable Twentieth-Century Scientists.* Detroit: Gale, 1995. For adult readers but includes a brief and not too technical biography of Díaz.

Books on Related Topics

Allaby, Michael. *Floods.* New York: Facts On File, 1997. Describes floods and their causes in great detail. Part of a series called Dangerous Weather.

———. *Hurricanes.* New York: Facts On File, 1997. Describes hurricanes and their causes.

Burroughs, William J. *Weather.* Sydney, Australia: The Nature Company/Time-Life, 1996. For young adults, includes section on El Niños. Well-illustrated with photographs, maps, charts.

Cole, Joanna. *The Magic School Bus Inside a Hurricane.* New York: Scholastic, 1995. Takes young readers on a word and picture journey into the heart of a hurricane.

Dineen, Jacqueline. *Hurricanes and Typhoons.* New York: Gloucester Press, 1991. Describes for young readers the creation and violence of hurricanes and typhoons.

Flagg, Ann. *Weather.* New York: Scholastic, 1997. A young adult book on the weather.

Kramer, Stephen P. *Eye of the Storm: Chasing Storms with Warren Faidley.* New York: Putnam's Sons, 1997. Exciting accounts of violent storms witnessed by stormtracker Faidley.

Peissel, Michel, and Missy Allen. *Dangerous Natural Phenomena.* New York: Chelsea House, 1993. Covers 24 weather-related types of catastrophes.

Twist, Clint. *Hurricanes and Storms.* New York: Dillon Press, 1992. Young readers' book with descriptions of violent storms.

Francisco Dallmeier, a wildlife biologist, is a leading plant and animal conservationist specializing in preserving the world's remaining rain forests. (Courtesy Smithsonian Institution)

Francisco Dallmeier

WILDLIFE BIOLOGIST
(1953–)

Venezuela-born Francisco Dallmeier, one of the world's leading wildlife biologists and plant and animal conservationists, was lost in a rain forest in mountainous southern Peru during a torrential storm in 1988. He was on an expedition from the Smithsonian Institution in Washington, D.C., to study and make a record of the plants and animals of the region.

Three other scientists with whom Dallmeier was traveling failed to return to the base camp and were presumed lost. Despite heavy rain, he joined two native guides in searching for his missing companions.

"Darkness began to fall over the rain forest and we realized that we, too, were lost," Dallmeier recalled, speaking about the experience later. "The guides decided to make a camp in the forest and try to put up some kind of shelter for the night."

The guides made a little shed out of tree branches and palm leaves, but they had no matches to light a fire. Dallmeier searched his pants pockets.

"Having flown my own plane in many remote parts of the world, I always take survival gear with me," Dallmeier said. "I had brought along a magnesium bar with which I lit the fire. The native guides thought I had produced magic out of my pocket."

Peru's rain forests are inhabited by mountain lions and jaguars, but if humans leave them alone, the cats usually won't harm them. What Dallmeier and his guides worried about more were poisonous snakes.

"While we were sleeping in the dark early hours of the morning, one of the guides woke up screaming," Dallmeier said. "He had taken off his rubber boots and socks, and a vampire bat had swooped down and bit his big toe. It bled and hurt, but the bite wasn't fatal."

By morning, the rain had stopped, and Dallmeier and his guides tried again to find their way back to the base camp. They were rescued about an hour's walk downriver from the camp, and Dallmeier learned that his lost companions had found their way safely back to the camp the night before, after only a few hours.

Later, speaking about how it felt to be lost overnight during a torrential storm in a rain forest with wild animals and snakes, Dallmeier recalled, "I didn't panic. I felt safe. Maybe it was because all my life, and in the work I do as a wildlife biologist and conservationist, I have been friendly to plants and animals and try to protect them. I guess I felt they would be friendly and protect me."

☆ ☆ ☆

Francisco Gómez-Dallmeier was born in Caracas, Venezuela, on February 15, 1953. His great-grandfather, the renowned German scientist and naturalist Adolph Ernst, had settled in Venezuela after the Nazis confiscated his property before the outbreak of World War II. Dallmeier's parents, Francisco and Ana Teresa Dallmeier, were born in Venezuela where his father became manager of a cancer research institute.

"At the age of three, I loved and was fascinated by nature and animals," said Dallmeier. "I knew I wanted to work like my great-grandfather had with animals and plants, and to discover many of nature's secrets."

While attending elementary and high school in Caracas, Dallmeier joined the Boy Scouts as a way to be outdoors and go camping. He wanted to become a member of the LaSalle Museum of Natural History in Caracas but was too young. However, when he turned 14, he was allowed to become a volunteer.

"I got all the nasty work," Dallmeier recalled.

> Cleaning smelly specimen cabinets, and boiling skulls of animals, to prepare them for the museum's collection. It was okay. I just did it.
>
> The work allowed me to dream and let my imagination fly into the world of nature. It enabled me to explore rare forms of life I had never seen before. It helped me to shape my future and develop a commitment to the natural world.

When he was 18, Dallmeier was appointed curator of mammals at the museum. Two years later, in 1973, while studying for a degree in biology from the Central University of Venezuela, he became the museum's director. At age 20, he was the youngest museum director in the world. He held the post until 1977 when he received a bachelor's degree in biology.

Also during his university years, Dallmeier was a research assistant for Central University's Institute of Tropical Zoology, taking jeep expeditions into the rain forests and flood plains to study the flora and fauna of the Amazon region and elsewhere in Venezuela. Besides identifying and recording the numbers of many species of plants and animals of the area, he helped band more than 3,000 birds for migratory monitoring purposes. He also conducted census studies of many populations of waterfowl, taken both on the ground and from a small airplane.

Dallmeier then worked four years for INELMECA, a private engineering company, and with Battelle Columbus Laboratories of Ohio, conducting the first environmental impact study for Venezuela following construction of the largest thermoelectric power plant for South America. Such a study involves analyzing and establishing the effects of a particular commercial activity on an area and inhabitants—the humans, plants, animals, birds, and fish that live there.

After four years, Dallmeier decided to go to graduate school in the United States to learn more about wildlife conservation and biodiversity. He describes biodiversity as, "How many species of plants and animals there are on earth, how they are organized and distributed in different environments, and how important they are to the environment—what kind of functions they provide."

One of Dallmeier's passions in life was to be a wildlife biologist. Wildlife biologists not only study plants and animals, they often work in the area of conservation biology, preventing habitat destruction and plant and animal species extinction. Dallmeier wanted to go to one of the best wildlife management schools, so he chose Colorado State University (CSU) in Fort Collins, Colorado.

"I was accepted with a scholarship," Dallmeier said, "but since classes would not start for several more months, I was sent to Tennessee to take a refresher course in English. I wanted to have a more active outdoor life while studying, so I spent my free time learning to fly a plane and got a pilot's license. I discovered I love to fly, and being a pilot of my own plane would help me to do aerial duck and other waterfowl research later."

Since the future is too difficult to predict entirely, the trick is to make strides toward achieving your dream until you get to a point of no return.

—Francisco Dallmeier

After graduating with a master's degree in biology in 1984 from CSU, Dallmeier began work toward a doctorate in wildlife ecology. The following year, a friend asked him a favor: to pick up some transcripts at the graduate school office. There Dallmeier met his future wife. Nancy Joy Parton, who had a degree in business administration, was in charge of the graduate school office. They married in 1985 and five years later had a daughter,

Dallmeier (right) inspects monkey bones at an Indian village in Bolivia while conducting conservation research in 1987. (Courtesy Smithsonian Institution)

Alina, and in 1992, a son, Julian. In 1988 Dallmeier became a U.S. citizen.

After receiving his doctorate degree in wildlife ecology from CSU in 1986, Dallmeier joined the staff of the Smithsonian Institution and helped plan its Man and the Biosphere biodiversity project, later becoming the project's director.

Dallmeier has had a lifelong concern for the effects that commercial destruction of the world's rain forests have on the plants and animals that live there. This led him to focus his career as wildlife biologist on the effects of human economic development on tropical areas.

"With a knowledge of biodiversity of life, we can not only protect remaining plants and animals from extinction but provide many more resources for human use," said Dallmeier.

> For instance, there are from 250,000 to 300,000 species of plants on earth, and of those, about 15,000 can be eaten by humans. But we are now using only from 150 to 200 of them. The rest are being destroyed by burning and cutting of forests all over the world, being replaced by what are called mono-cultures. These are areas that are set aside for a single use, such as rice, corn, or wheat fields. These can help feed the world's human population, but such single use of vast areas changes the once complex and interdependent environment into a very simple one.
>
> Where commercial use of an area dominates, hundreds of lifeforms are being killed off, not only animals and plants, but even microscopic life. If we destroy the rainforests, we lose those lifeforms. But because of their medicinal and food source potential, they can be important for human use.

Dallmeier estimates that over the next 25 years, more than a million species of plants and animals may become extinct. Most of these extinctions will occur in the tropics, where the pressure of native poverty and population growth and a lack of technical and scientific assistance make conservation efforts extremely difficult. Such efforts are often further hampered by the lack of basic information on the biological resources that are most in need of protection. Dallmeier maintains that long-term forest inventories are one means of obtaining such information.

From 1987 to 1991, Dallmeier developed procedures for establishing permanent forest inventory and monitoring plots at field sites

*Dallmeier uses a power computer to record and study his research as director of a
biological diversity program at the Smithsonian Institution in Washington, D.C.*
(Courtesy Smithsonian Institution)

FRANCISCO DALLMEIER

Teenagers can help us save our forests and the wildlife that live there by becoming involved in conservation and natural resources management. We don't have enough human resources to obtain and process the information we need to advise governments in how to conserve what is left of our forests and their wildlife.

Dallmeier said teens can get started in this effort by taking part in any local conservation or nature activity. They can join the Boy or Girl Scouts to learn about the environment they have right in their own community. They can volunteer to help conservationist organizations and protest to local officials about the use of pesticides on the lawns in their neighborhood.

"Teens can start creating their own environmental health monitoring plan right in their own backyard," Dallmeier said. "They can help a lot to prevent the use of destructive, poisonous technologies on the plants and animals in their own towns and cities. It's like a doctor taking their temperature and blood pressure to measure their health. Teens can discover what is the health of the environment where they live."

In 1997, Dallmeier spent four months globe-trotting on behalf of the biodiversity of life on Earth. His travels took him to Southeast Asia, then to Switzerland for an international meeting to conduct environmental monitoring in European forests, and then to West Africa for similar work. Before returning home to his family in Annandale, Virginia, and his desk at the Smithsonian in Washington, Dallmeier attended a meeting in Bolivia on the 10 years of research on the Amazon's lowland rain forests.

> T*he only way to preserve our natural resources is if conservationists and loggers, miners, oil companies, and others work together for shared sustainable use and management of what's left.*
>
> —Francisco Dallmeier

Dallmeier loves animals, such as the spider monkey he played with during a field trip in Bolivia. (Courtesy Smithsonian Institution)

With all his travels around the world, Dallmeier said he did not encounter obstacles from his Venezuelan birth and Hispanic heritage. On the contrary, they have helped him to communicate better with people of other origins, especially those he speaks to and works with in the developing countries of the world.

When not worrying about the health of the plants and animals of the world, Dallmeier tries to find time for his hobbies, which include photography, swimming, scuba diving, camping, and flying.

Dallmeier also actively encourages young people in their search for a meaningful career and life. "Sometimes, it looks like there is no hope," he said. "But if you create a vision, or dream, of what you want to achieve, and develop your objective, you'll get it. I've had to work hard, and never give up. Almost always, whatever I dream to achieve, I get it. Try it. It works."

Chronology

February 15, 1953	Francisco Gómez-Dallmeier is born in Caracas, Venezuela
1971	becomes curator of mammals, LaSalle Museum of Natural History, Caracas
1973	becomes the museum's director
1973–77	serves as research assistant with Central University of Venezuela's Institute of Tropical Zoology and continues as museum director
1977	receives bachelor's degree in biology from Central University of Venezuela
1977–81	coordinates ecological program for INEL-MECA, a Venezuelan environmental engineering company, and Battelle Columbus Laboratories, Ohio
1984	earns master's degree in wildlife biology from Colorado State University, Fort Collins, Colorado
1985	marries Nancy Joy Parton
1986	earns doctorate in wildlife ecology from Colorado State University
1986–88	is manager of Smithsonian Institution's Man and the Biosphere Biological Diversity Program
1988	becomes U.S. citizen
1989–present	is director of Smithsonian biodiversity project
1995	establishes and conducts first "Tree Watch" project

is editor of *Forest Biodiversity Research, Monitoring, and Modeling*

Further Reading

Book by Francisco Dallmeier
Dallmeier, Francisco, and J. A. Comiskey. *Forest Biodiversity Research, Monitoring, and Modeling.* New York: Pantheon Press, 1997. Scientific book intended for adult reading.

Books about Francisco Dallmeier
Kanellos, Nicholas. *Hispanic-American Almanac.* Detroit: Gale, 1993. Brief, readable biography on Dallmeier.
McMurray, Emily J. *Notable Twentieth-Century Scientists.* Detroit: Gale, 1995. Adult book, but biography on Dallmeier is easy to understand.

Books on Related Topics
Alvin, Virginia, and Silverstein, Robert. *Saving Endangered Animals.* Hillside, N.J.: Enslow, 1993. Good young adult reading on wildlife conservation.
Dalton, Stephen. *Vanishing Paradise: The Tropical Rainforest.* Woodstory, N.Y.: Overlook Press, 1990. For young readers, describes the remaining rainforests as endangered habitats.
Fanning, Odom. *Opportunities in Environmental Careers.* Lincolnwood, Ill.: VGM Career Horizons, 1995. Young adult book about careers in wildlife biology and other environmental fields.
Gallant, Roy A. *Earth's Vanishing Forests.* New York: Macmillan, 1991. Young adult book about forest conservation.
Langone, John. *Our Endangered Earth: What We Can Do to Save It.* Boston: Little, Brown, 1992. Young adult book about the environment with chapters on deforestation and endangered wildlife.

Adriana Ocampo, a planetary geologist at the Jet Propulsion Laboratory of the Califor-
nia Institute of Technology, is part of a team of scientists who are probing outer space
by way of NASA shuttle missions to Jupiter, Mars, and other planets. (Courtesy Jet
Propulsion Laboratory)

Adriana Ocampo

PLANETARY GEOLOGIST
(1955–)

A driana Ocampo was lecturing about the U.S. Mars mission to
Spanish-speaking visitors at the Jet Propulsion Laboratory (JPL)
in Pasadena, California, on July 4, 1997, when the news broke. She
and other scientists and engineers working at mission control of the
National Aeronautics and Space Administration (NASA) could
hardly contain their excitement when they learned that the United
States's *Pathfinder* spacecraft had landed on Mars.

NASA's first trip to Mars in 21 years was a huge success. The U.S.
space program had taken a giant step toward learning if there is or
could be life on the distant planet. Ocampo, a Colombian-born
American planetary geologist, was among the JPL scientists who
eagerly awaited photos of the planet's surface from *Pathfinder*'s probe,
an explorer robot named Sojourner that looked like a little red wagon.
Shortly after the Sojourner touched down onto Mars, its robotic arm
with a flexible "wrist" placed the sensor in contact with rocks and

soil, and it began transmitting televised photos back to Earth that astonished even Ocampo and other JPL scientists.

"It was fabulous!" Ocampo said later in an interview. "The pictures show us that Mars has a much more diversified landscape than we had expected. That tells us the planet has a much more complicated geological history. As a planetary geologist, that really excites me!" A planetary geologist studies the rocks, soil, and other natural features of planets. "The Mars landing was an incredible event!"

☆ ☆ ☆

Adriana Christian Ocampo was born January 5, 1955, in Barranquilla, Colombia, in northwest South America. Her father, Victor, is an engineer and her mother, Teresa, is a school teacher. When Adriana was just a few months old, her parents moved far south and settled in Buenos Aires, the chief port and capital of Argentina.

"As a girl I was more interested in a chemistry set than in dolls," Ocampo recalled. "And I was always fascinated by the stars. My mother says I wouldn't go to sleep without going out and seeing the night sky. I've never lost that sense of wonder about the stars, the planets, and outer space."

The family immigrated to the United States in 1970 so that Adriana, then 15, and her two sisters could get a better education. They settled in Pasadena, California. High school aptitude tests that Adriana had taken in Argentina had indicated she might consider a career in business or accounting. But she became interested in physics and calculus and convinced school counselors in Pasadena to let her study for a science career.

"I always had an inquisitive mind," Ocampo recalled, "and tried to understand how things work. America's space program, especially when we put the first human on the moon in 1969, excited me tremendously."

During her junior year in high school in 1973, Ocampo worked part-time at NASA's Jet Propulsion Laboratory in Pasadena compiling data for a study of polar motion.

Ocampo majored in aerospace engineering at Pasadena City College and continued working part-time at the JPL doing basic electrical engineering for a study of earthquakes. In her junior year she took part in a science program sponsored by JPL.

While in college in 1980 she became a U.S. citizen. She left Pasadena City College and entered California State University at Los Angeles where she received her bachelor of science degree in geology in 1983. Upon graduation, she accepted a full-time position at JPL.

*S*pace exploration *is a great vehicle for education.*

—Adriana Ocampo

Ocampo's abilities as a planetary geologist were soon put to test when she was assigned to the imaging team of NASA's Viking mission. Her job was to plan the observations of the Martian moons Phobos and Deimos. This work culminated in a NASA publication of a Phobos atlas in 1984 and the search for a ring and satellites of Mars, which was utilized in the Soviet Union's Phobos mission.

During the Voyager mission to the outer planets, Ocampo worked on the navigation and mission planning team, including the development of an ephemeris for Saturn. An ephemeris is an astronomical calendar showing the positions of a heavenly body on specific dates and over an extended period of time. Ocampo also worked in the JPL Multi-mission Image Processing Laboratory where she developed an expertise in image processing, image visualization, and analysis using computers.

Ocampo then became science coordinator for separate sensing instruments on two of NASA's and the JPL's subsequent major planetary projects—the Mars Observer and Project Galileo missions.

In the Mars Observer Project, NASA's first Mars venture in 17 years, Ocampo was the scientist responsible for the unmanned spacecraft's thermal emission spectrometer—an instrument used to measure the heat produced by the planet that enabled cartographers (mapmakers) to create more accurate maps of Mars.

Unfortunately, the mission failed in 1993 when after an 11-month journey, the spacecraft fell silent for no apparent reason. It then spun out of control due to a malfunction and never finished its flight to Mars; the spectrometer Ocampo had been working on remained untested.

Ocampo uses computer, video, and other technology to follow sequencing and commanding of NASA's Galileo *spacecraft on its reconnaissance mission to Jupiter.* (Courtesy Jet Propulsion Laboratory)

Ocampo is currently working in Flight Projects Mission Operations as the science coordinator to the Near-Infrared Mapping Spectrometer (NIMS), an instrument that is part of NASA's Galileo mission to Jupiter. She is responsible for science observations and analysis.

Launched in 1989, the *Galileo* spacecraft was named after the Italian Renaissance scientist who discovered Jupiter's major moons in 1610 with the first astronomical telescope. During its six-year path to Jupiter, the spacecraft traveled past Venus once, Earth twice, and made two passes through the asteroid belt, which provided flybys of the asteroids Gaspra and Ida.

The *Galileo,* consisting of two principal parts—an orbiter and an atmospheric probe—arrived at Jupiter on December 7, 1995. It then fired its main engine for a successful orbit around the planet. The craft's atmospheric probe plunged into Jupiter's atmosphere and relayed information on the structure and composition of the solar system's largest planet. It began a multi-year stint orbiting Jupiter, which it continues to do today, returning a steady stream of images and scientific data on the planet and its moons. The first two encounters were successfully performed with Jupiter's largest moon, Ganymede, on June 27 and September 6, 1996.

The Galileo mission revealed in 1997 that Jupiter has both wet and dry regions, just as Earth has tropics and deserts. The data may explain why Galileo's atmospheric probe found much less water in one part of the planet, in the Jovian atmosphere, than scientists had anticipated. During its voyage, the *Galileo* also transmitted back to scientists photos of Earth, the Moon, Venus, and the crater-pocked asteroid Gaspra. Ocampo was assigned to oversee the operation of the NIMS mounted on NASA's *Galileo* spacecraft. As one of four remote sensing instruments attached to the space probe, NIMS was to measure reflected sunlight and heat from Jupiter's atmosphere.

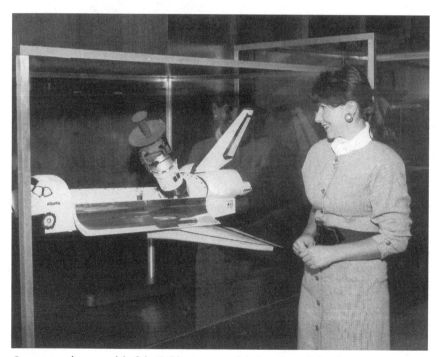

Ocampo studies a model of the Galileo *spacecraft before the real ship begins its space shuttle journey to Jupiter.* (Courtesy Jet Propulsion Laboratory)

ADRIANA OCAMPO

The data would help scientists to determine the planet's composition, cloud structure, and temperature. With the information gathered by NIMS, scientists would begin to learn more about the surface chemistry and mineral composition of Jupiter's four moons.

Ocampo's NIMS instrument scanned the asteroid's surface as it flew past in 1991 and revealed valuable new information. The images indicated that Gaspra is covered by a soil-like substance of pulverized rock and dust thinner than that of the Moon's surface. The Galileo Mission's photos of Gaspra were the world's first close-up images of an asteroid.

Science education is a special interest of Ocampo's. In 1987 Ocampo organized a course in planetary sciences that was taught in

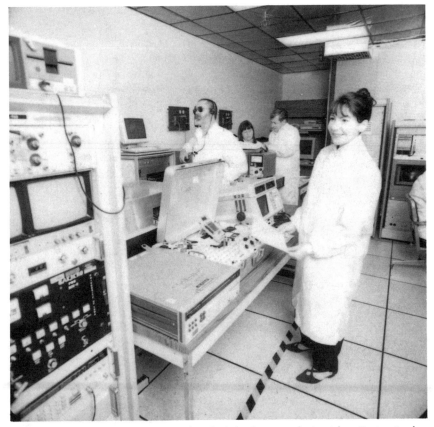

Ocampo with the NIMS instrument that she helped prepare for its ride to Jupiter in the Galileo *spacecraft* (Courtesy Jet Propulsion Laboratory)

Mexico City under the sponsorship of The Planetary Society. The course, the first of its kind, proved so successful in disseminating information that the United Nations, in conjunction with the European Space Agency and The Planetary Society, funded similar workshops in Costa Rica and Colombia in 1992, Nigeria in 1993, and Egypt in 1994. Ocampo was a major force in developing the format and character of the workshops, which helped promote scientific and educational cooperation in space science between developing and developed countries.

The Mars photos were exciting beyond our expectations.

—Adriana Ocampo

Ocampo also was instrumental in developing the concept for the Space Conference for the Americas: Prospects in Cooperation, held in Costa Rica in 1990. Developed in conjunction with the United Nations, the conference was designed to encourage cooperation in science and technology for peaceful uses of space and for improving the quality of life among Pan-American nations. Continuing this effort, Ocampo helped organize the Second Space Conference of the Americas, held in Chile in 1993. She still serves on an international advisory board for this effort.

Since 1988, Ocampo also has been active in geological research. She was the first scientist to recognize that a ring of cenotes, or sinkholes, found in the Yucatán peninsula was related to the buried impact crater called Chicxulub. It is believed that the impact caused the extinction of 50 percent of animals living on Earth, including the dinosaurs, at the end of the Cretaceous period, 65 million years ago. These studies, conducted while working at JPL, allowed Ocampo to complete in 1997 her master of science degree in geology at California State University at Northridge.

Ocampo is a member of a scientific consortium between Mexico and the United States to study the origin of the Chicxulub crater. She was awarded a NASA grant to continue her research on the effects the impact had on the earth's biosphere and how it relates to dinosaurs' extinction. Also in 1997, Ocampo was selected as a coinvestigator in the Hermes mission to explore the planet Mercury.

ADRIANA OCAMPO

Hermes is part of NASA's Discovery Program, a new series of low-cost planetary missions.

Ocampo has been active in Hispanic-American education and working with Hispanic-American engineers and other professionals. Her efforts have taken her to Germany, Nigeria, Egypt, Sri Lanka, Mexico, Costa Rica, Colombia, Honduras, Uruguay, and other countries.

She served on the Society of Hispanic Professional Engineers (SHPE) national board of directors for three years, the first of these as national secretary and the second two as the national vice president. She has also served in SHPE's International Affairs Committee as chairperson establishing technical programs of cooperation and university student exchange between the United States and Mexico.

Ocampo is a member of the Association of Women in Geoscience, the American Institute of Aeronautics and Astronautics, the Society of Women Engineers where she is a strong supporter of a program mentoring young girls, and many other professional organizations. As a member of the JPL Speakers Bureau she has represented the NASA agency in various speaking engagements in both English and Spanish held both in the United States and in many Latin countries, promoting space science and engineering. In 1992 she was awarded the Woman of the Year Award in Science by the Comisión Femenil, a Los Angeles–based organization that educates and promotes Hispanic women. In 1994 she was the only scientist selected by JPL to represent the agency at the Leadership Conference for Women in Science and Engineering in Washington, D.C. She has coauthored many articles and scientific papers on her work in both space and archaeology.

In 1996 Ocampo was awarded the JPL's Advisory Council for Women Award for outreach and community work. In 1997 she received a science and technology award from the Chicano Federation for her contribution to science.

In March 1998 Ocampo was transferred to NASA headquarters in Washington, D.C., to work as a program executive representing the United States in an international space science program. She assists in developing scientific collaborations with scientists from Europe, Russia, Japan, and other countries whose mutual aim is to learn more about phenomenon, such as black holes, that can provide more knowledge about space to be shared among nations. One such project she is engaged in is between NASA and its Japanese equivalent to learn new sources of X-ray astronomy, which can be helpful in the study of satellites and black holes.

Ocampo says she is lucky because her hobby is her work. She also loves to fly; she is a student pilot and has applied to become a space shuttle mission specialist. Ocampo is married to Kevin O. Pope, a geologist and archaeologist who works for a company that does remote-sensing geological and ecological research.

Ocampo advises young people, "Follow your dreams and passions. Be true to your heart and live life with gusto. And never give up."

Chronology

JANUARY 5, 1955	Adriana Christian Ocampo is born in Barranquilla, Colombia; family moves to Buenos Aires, Argentina
1970	immigrates to Pasadena, California
1973	starts working part-time for Jet Propulsion Laboratory (JPL)
1980	becomes U.S. citizen
1983	receives bachelor of science degree in geology from California State University at Los Angeles; begins full-time work for JPL
1984	produces photo atlas of one of the moons of Mars; becomes a science coordinator on Mars Observer mission
1989	oversees operation of mapping instrument on spacecraft for Project Galileo
1990	originates Space Conference for the Americas

1990–PRESENT	continues planetary geology work for Jet Propulsion Laboratory
1997	receives master of science degree in geology from California State University; is selected as coinvestigator in Hermes mission to Mercury
1998	transfers to NASA's Washington, D.C. headquarters; works as program executive in international space science program

Further Reading

Books and Articles about Adriana Ocampo

Leiva, Miriam, editor. *Geometry Explorations and Applications.* Evanston, Ill.: McDougal & Littell, 1998. Brief biography of Ocampo as mathematician and scientist.

McMurray, Emily J. *Notable Twentieth-Century Scientists.* Detroit: Gale, 1995. Brief biography of Ocampo.

Mellado, Carmela. "Adriana Ocampo." *Hispanic Engineer* (Fall 1987). Short biography of Ocampo.

———. "The Women Leaders of the SHPE National Board of Directors." *Hispanic Engineer* (Fall 1989). Brief biography of Ocampo.

Recipes for Success. Boston: Patriots Trail Girl Scout Council, 1997. Includes a page about Ocampo and one of her favorite dessert recipes. Available by calling 1-800-882-1662.

Women of Hope/Latinas Abriendo Camino. Video and poster with biography of Ocampo. Available from Bread and Roses Cultural Project, 330 West 42nd Street, Seventh Floor, New York, New York 10036.

Books and Information on Related Topics

Apfel, Necia H. *Voyager to the Planets.* New York: Clarion, 1991. Young person's guide to NASA's Voyager expeditions to the solar system.

Beebe, Reta. *Jupiter: the Giant Planet.* Washington: Smithsonian Institution Press, 1994. Adult book about Jupiter, but young adults should find it a good, readable source of information.

Burrows, William E. *Mission to Deep Space: Voyager's Journey of Discovery.* New York: Freeman, 1993. Juvenile book describing America's Voyager space missions.

Cattermole, Peter John. *Earth and Other Planets: Geology and Space Research.* New York: Oxford University Press, 1995. Adult book teens will find readable on studies of the geology of Earth and other nearby planets.

Corrick, James A. *Mars.* New York: Watts, 1991. Good young adult book on the planet Mars.

McDonald, Mary Ann. *Jupiter.* Mankato, Minn.: Child's World, 1993. Spanish-language book for young readers about the red planet.

Wiggers, Raymond. *The Amateur Geologist: Explorations and Investigations.* Danbury, Conn.: Watts, 1993. A guide to geology projects and geological sites in the United States.

Teachers and students can keep up with continuing news about NASA's and JPL's Jupiter mission by visiting JPL's on-line website at http://www.jpl.nasa.gov/galileo/ or by addressing e-mail to NASA at listmanager@quest.arc.nasa.gov. For information on the Mars Pathfinder Mission, go to http://www.jpl.nasa.gov/mpfmir.

Margarita Colmenares, a leading advocate of education, worked as an environmental engineer for the Chevron Corporation before becoming director of the Office of Corporate Liaisons at the U.S. Department of Education in Washington, D.C. (Courtesy U.S. Department of Education)

Margarita Colmenares

ENVIRONMENTAL ENGINEER
(1957–)

Margarita Colmenares, one of America's most accomplished environmental engineers and leading education advocates, discovered engineering by accident. While in high school, she was directed by her counselors to take courses in typing, shorthand, and adding machines because she was "not smart enough to take algebra."

"During my sophomore year in college, I was on a 'date' in the library," she recalled in an interview. "My boyfriend had all his books spread out on a table. He was so totally absorbed in them that I leaned over to see what he was studying.

"I read a word problem that required trying to figure out the thrust and acceleration of a space shuttle rocket. I flipped the cover of the book which had the word 'physics' on it and naively asked, 'What is physics?' He explained to me that physics was one of the courses required for engineering. My next question was 'What is engineering?'"

What Colmenares learned from that experience prompted her to switch her major from business to engineering, and she went on to graduate from Stanford University with an engineering degree. Since then she has become a leading environmental engineer, working in both industry and education.

☆ ☆ ☆

Margarita Hortensia Colmenares was born in Sacramento, California, on July 20, 1957, the eldest of five brothers and sisters. Her parents—Luis Colmenares, a laborer, and Hortensia Colmenares—had come to the United States from Mexico a few years earlier in search of a better life for themselves and their future family.

The Colmenares settled in a part of Sacramento where many other immigrant families lived. Luis Colmenares joined others as migrant workers picking strawberries, peaches, and tomatoes on farms in the Sacramento Valley. Later he worked in a cannery and then a warehouse while his wife worked in a department store.

"Even though both my parents worked, our family needed to generate extra income, so my brothers and sisters and I all pitched in to deliver newspapers and sell jewelry and Avon and Tupperware products," Colmenares recalled in an interview for *No Universal Constants: Journeys of Women in Science and Engineering.*

"My parents encouraged us all to work and study hard and to make good use of the nearby library. I loved to read so much, I made my poor eyesight worse because I refused to put a book down until I finished reading it, even if it meant continuing to read by moonlight or with a flashlight under the covers." She learned to read so well that when she was in the second grade, she was selected to help tutor other children in reading.

The summer after her sophomore year in high school, Colmenares was hired by the local branch of the Xerox Corporation, which had started a community outreach program to hire four inner-city youths. She worked hard and was rewarded with more responsibilities. At the age of 17, she was entrusted to develop a customer care program. She developed a process to survey and track customer satisfaction levels, which were then reported to management.

Eager to go to college, during the first half of her senior year in high school Colmenares was allowed to also take classes at the local community college. By the end of the second half of her senior year in high school, she was also a full-time student at the local community college. After meeting the admission requirements at California State University in Sacramento, she enrolled there as a business major.

In her sophomore year, Colmenares convinced the dean of the School of Engineering to let her change her major so that she could become an engineer. Engineering is the application of the properties of matter and the sources of energy in nature to practical purposes, such as machines and structures.

Colmenares took chemistry, physics, and other introductory engineering classes. While at California State University, she worked as an engineering student assistant in the Department of Water Resources, an agency of California State. As part of a project surveillance team, she assessed the structural integrity of the state's aqueduct system at regular intervals and especially right after earthquakes. Her job was to conduct structural inspections, interpret data, and write technical reports.

After a year, she returned to the community college so that she could compete for a General Electric scholarship for women and minorities. She won and it paid for up to 80 percent of her tuition and books. While at the community college, Colmenares was awarded its highest honor, the Distinguished Service Award. Her name is permanently engraved on a bronze plaque at the entrance to the college.

Colmenares then applied to Stanford University in Palo Alto as a transfer student and was accepted. While there, she continued her community work, which she had begun as a teenager. She tutored children in East Palo Alto, an area of poverty and unemployment near the university. She also found time to teach Mexican folk dance and codirect the Stanford Ballet Folklórico.

Colmenares graduated from Stanford with a degree in civil engineering in 1981 and began her career with the Chevron Corporation. Civil engineering concerns the planning, designing, construction, and maintenance of structures and the altering of geography to suit the needs of a building project.

Over the next 10 years, Colmenares lived in 10 different cities, working in engineering jobs of increasing responsibility for Chevron. "My first engineering job, in 1979, was making unleaded gasoline at the Chevron refinery in El Paso, Texas," she recalled. "I had to become familiar with the Rheniformer, which is a 200-foot [61-meter] tower that contains a catalyst which turns 'straight run' gasoline into unleaded. This required an understanding of chemistry and the effects of temperature and high pressures."

Working as a field engineer in 1981 as part of a preventative environmental program, she had to replace underground steel tanks with fiberglass tanks before they started to leak. She worked with computer models that predicted the lifespan of steel tanks depending on their age and the type of soil they were placed in. She used her knowledge of statistics and geology to prioritize which service stations should be done first.

Colmenares became a foreign training liaison representative for Chevron in 1983 and set up training assignments for engineers from Saudi Arabia, Indonesia, Venezuela, and other countries. In 1985, she became an environmental compliance specialist for Chevron in Houston, Texas. By 1987 she was the lead engineer for an $18 million environmental cleanup project for the Chevron refinery in El Segundo, near Los Angeles. Her team was responsible for the design and construction of the subsurface, the injection system, and the water treatment facilities to remove hydrocarbons from the groundwater.

In 1989, as a Chevron air quality specialist, she had to calculate the amount of refinery air emissions and identify process changes that could reduce air emissions and associated costs. She used her computer programming skills to modify the computer model that was being used at the time.

Meanwhile, all during her engineering career, Colmenares found time for continuing her community service. Upon graduation from Stanford, she organized and was elected founding president of the San Francisco chapter of the Society of Hispanic Professional Engineers (SHPE), a nonprofit volunteer organization. It provides role models, financial assistance, and inspiration to aspiring Hispanic-American engineering students. Over the next 10 years, she served

Colmenares (second from left), who has won awards for her commitment to community and national service, frequently visits elementary and high schools to see students' science exhibits and encourage them to pursue careers in science. (Courtesy U.S. Department of Education)

in various leadership positions for the organization and was elected its national president. According to Colmenares, she was the first female to head the group of more than 10,000 volunteers. As national president of SHPE, Colmenares met thousands of engineering students, parents, counselors, and corporate representatives.

"All my life, I've encountered people who are either surprised or curious that I'm an engineer," Colmenares said. "One such incident occurred at a construction site across from Golden Gate Park in San Francisco. I was supervising a crew that was replacing the underground storage steel tanks with fiberglass tanks."

Local fire and safety regulations required sign-offs by the fire marshal before finishing the job. I was waiting for the fire marshal, who was late, when all of a sudden a red car screeched onto the work site. The fire marshal, a rather large man, emerged and started walking very quickly past me, even though I was standing at the edge of this very large hole in the ground. He moved towards an older man standing by the office, yelling out, "Where's the engineer?" The other man pointed to me and said, "She's right there." The fire marshal wheeled around on his heels and exclaimed, astonished, "You're the engineer?"

At other times, Colmenares found it necessary to gain the confidence of others. When one of my job assignments took me to Utah," she recalled,

on the plane ride from Denver my male colleague turned to me halfway through the flight and said, "You know, I just don't understand why they're sending you to replace me." When I naively asked, "What do you mean?" he replied, "Well, you're a woman and you're a Hispanic."

Up to that point, I didn't think I had given it any real consideration, but his comment made me realize that up in that part of the country, I probably would be the first professional woman engineer sent to supervise construction crews. Sure enough, the men were quick to size me up. They tried to get away with shortcuts on the specifications, but I held my ground.

Inspired by IBM (International Business Machines) programs in which executives are loaned to take part in educational projects, Colmenares wrote a proposal describing the need for Chevron to make an investment in human capital by loaning her full-time to SHPE. She compared it with the company's current investments in oil fields, spending vast amounts of money in order to yield future long-term dividends. After approval by the board of directors, she became a Chevron executive-on-loan, enabling her to work full-time for SHPE while being reimbursed by Chevron for salary and travel expenses.

R*emember the past,*
live the present,
trust the future.

—Margarita Colmenares

Following her second year as SHPE national president, Colmenares was selected as the first Hispanic engineer to become a White House fellow. Fellows are selected for outstanding leadership ability, professional excellence, intellectual ability, character, and commitment to community and national service, and are given one-year assignments at the White House or a cabinet agency.

Colmenares was assigned to work with David Kearns, then deputy secretary of education and former chief executive officer of the Xerox Corporation. It gave her special pleasure to tell him that working for his company during college had helped develop her communication, presentation, and teamwork skills.

As a White House fellow, Colmenares worked with an interagency council on math and science education. Its purpose was to review and coordinate federal spending on the programs by 16 federal agencies including the National Aeronautics and Space Administration (NASA), the National Science Foundation, the Smithsonian Institution, and the Department of Education. After her White House Fellowship, she returned to Chevron to take on an international marketing assignment in Latin America.

In 1993, the summer following President Bill Clinton's election, Colmenares was appointed director of corporate liaisons for the U.S. Department of Education and was in that position at the time of this interview in 1997. Her job was to work with business leaders and organizations from across the United States and try to engage their support for education.

Colmenares established a chief executive officer steering group in support of the Clinton administration's efforts to increase family-friendly practices in the workplace. She recruited business, community, and education leaders to identify effective strategies, share best practices, and make best use of resources. She also provided advice and technical guidance to private and public partnership efforts in areas such as environmental education, improvement of math and science education, and helping young people in their transition from school to the workplace.

"There is an incredible need to help young people understand what awaits them in the working world," Colmenares said. "During a visit to a high school calculus class, I shared examples of engineering projects I had managed. As we talked through some of the problems I solved as an engineer, one student suddenly waved his arms excitedly as he pointed to all the math equations on the classroom walls and proclaimed, 'So that's why we need to learn all this stuff!'"

Colmenares not only believes the corporate community can be a very positive influence in educating young people about the workplace, she says parents also can and should play their part.

"My parents were constantly saying, '*Tú vas a ir al colegio!*'— 'You're going to go to college!'—even though they had never been to college. I am a product of the 'whole village' working together to educate a child. Without all of the components working together—my parents, caring teachers, business mentors, and my

Colmenares (fourth from left) believes it is important to prepare young people for their future careers by taking a strong interest in their school work, whether it be in science or any other subject. (Courtesy U.S. Department of Education)

community activities, I would not be where I am today."

Having taught Mexican folk dance as a young woman, dance still plays an important role in Colmenares's life. "I absolutely love dancing!" she said. Since coming to Washington, D.C., Colmenares has been involved in teaching dance to adults and children.

She has received many honors and awards. In 1989 she was named Outstanding Hispanic Woman of the Year by *Hispanic* magazine and also received *Hispanic Engineer* magazine's Community Service Award. That same year she also was named Hispanic Role Model of the Year by SHPE. In both 1990 and 1992, *Hispanic Business* magazine named her one of the 100 most influential Hispanics in the United States. In 1991, she was the youngest recipient ever to receive the California Community College League's Outstanding Alumni Award.

Colmenares often speaks to minority students at high schools, encouraging them to pursue challenging careers. "Unfortunately, the majority of Hispanic women do not have the opportunity to become prepared with the knowledge and skills to work in high technology fields such as engineering," she said.

On more than one occasion, as Colmenares has switched from engineering to work in education, she has been asked, "What is an engineer doing at the Department of Education?"

"I am an engineer, a businesswoman, and now a public servant," Colmenares replies. "But I am also a mentor, a role model, and an educator for the next generation. Their success is my success, which reminds me of a Malaysian education saying: 'Those who know a lot must teach those who know less. And those who know less must teach those who know nothing.'"

As director of corporate liaisons for the U.S. Department of Education, when lecturing to students, teachers, and corporate executives, Colmenares's closing words are always, "Better education is everybody's business!"

> **G**o where no man or woman has gone before.
>
> —Margarita Colmenares

Chronology

JULY 20, 1957	Margarita Hortensia Colmenares is born in Sacramento, California
1980–1981	before graduation from Stanford, takes nine months to work for Chevron at refinery in El Paso, Texas, and marketing operations in San Francisco
1981	graduates with bachelor of science degree in civil engineering from Stanford University; joins Chevron as a field construction engineer
1982	becomes founding president of San Francisco chapter of the Society of Hispanic Professional Engineers (SHPE)
1983	becomes Chevron's foreign training representative
1985	becomes environmental compliance specialist for Chevron in Houston, Texas
1987	becomes lead engineer of Chevron's environmental cleanup project at refinery in El Segundo, California
1989	becomes first woman elected national president, SHPE
1991–92	becomes first Hispanic engineer appointed a White House fellowship, assigned to U.S. Department of Education
1992–93	becomes marketing advisor for Chevron International
1993–PRESENT	serves as corporate liaison for U.S. Department of Education

Further Reading

Books about Margarita Colmenares

Ambrose, Susan, ed. *No Universal Constants: Journeys of Women in Science and Engineering.* Philadelphia: Temple University Press, 1997. Colmenares, among other women, tell personal accounts of their careers in their own words.

McMurray, Emily J. *Notable Twentieth-Century Scientists.* Detroit: Gale, 1995. Adult book but Colmenares biography is easy to understand.

Telgen, Diane, and Jim Kamp. *Notable Hispanic-American Women.* Detroit: Gale, 1993. Adult book containing a readable biography of Colmenares.

Books on Related Topics

Fanning, Odom. *Opportunities in Environmental Careers.* Lincolnwood, Ill.: VGM Career Horizons, 1996. Young adults learn about environmental careers including civil engineering.

Jakobson, Cathryn. *Think About the Environment.* New York: Walker, 1992. Young adult overview about the environment.

Langone, John. *Our Endangered Earth: What We Can Do to Save It.* Boston: Little, Brown, 1992. Young adult book on the environment.

Ellen Ochoa was born May 10, 1958, in Los Angeles, California, the third of five children of Joseph and Rosanne Ochoa. She grew up in La Mesa where her father, who was born in California of Mexican descent, was manager of a retail store. Her mother, also American-born, encouraged all five of her children to get a college education and excel in any field of work they chose.

Ochoa was a good student but did exceptionally well in math and science. At the age of 13, she won the San Diego County spelling bee. In junior high school, she was named the outstanding girl.

Valedictorian of her class, Ochoa graduated from Grossmont High School in La Mesa in 1975. While she was an excellent student and had a strong interest in research, she could not decide on what career to pursue. At San Diego State University she changed her major five times, from music to business to journalism to computer science, and finally to physics. She received a bachelor of science degree in 1980, also as valedictorian of her class.

Ochoa was then granted a Stanford University Engineering Fellowship for the year 1980–81 and earned a master of science degree in 1981. "During graduate work, I became excited about America's space program," Ochoa said in an interview. "When friends applied to NASA, I began considering a career as an astronaut."

She received an IBM (International Business Machines) Predoctoral Fellowship and got her doctorate in electrical engineering from Stanford in 1985. Electrical engineering involves the generation and transmission of electrical power and all the devices that use it.

While Ochoa had been doing graduate work, the U.S. space program was in high gear. In April 1981, the *Columbia,* the world's first reusable spacecraft, completed the first flight of the United States's proposed series of space shuttles. In June 1983, Sally Ride became the first American woman astronaut.

A space shuttle is a reusable spacecraft that is launched into orbit by rockets and then glides down to the earth's surface. It can carry telescopes, cameras, and a wide range of other research equipment.

In 1985, Ochoa became a member of the technical staff in the Imaging Technology Division at Sandia National Laboratories in

Livermore, California. One of Ochoa's brothers learned how to fly an airplane, and it inspired her to get her pilot's license for small engine planes in 1986. Ochoa put into action her dreams of becoming an astronaut two years later by joining NASA's Ames Research Center at Moffett Field, California. She was put in charge of work on optical recognition systems for space automation.

After only six months, Ochoa was selected as a group leader in the photonic processing group of the Intelligent Systems Technology Branch at Ames. She became technical and administrative leader of 35 engineers and scientists engaged in researching optical-image and data-processing techniques for space-based robotics. After six months, she became chief of the Intelligent Systems Technology Branch. In 1989 she received the Hispanic Engineer National Achievement Award for Most Promising Engineer in Government.

The following year, Ochoa married Coe Fulmer Miles. He was a computer research engineer working at NASA when they met and has since gone on to study law and work for a patent law firm. Their home is in La Mesa, California.

Also in 1990, Ochoa was selected by NASA to become an astronaut. After more than a year of intensive study and training, she became one in July 1991, but she had to wait two more years for a ride in space. That opportunity came in April 1993 when she was assigned to the crew of Discovery shuttle mission STS-56 (Space Transportation System, Flight 56). The shuttle's mission was to conduct atmospheric and solar studies in order to better understand the effect of solar activity on Earth's climate and environment.

Ochoa was responsible for the mission's primary payload, a Spartan 201 Satellite. Her job was to use a robotic arm to deploy and later retrieve the small, 2,800-pound (1,271-kg) satellite. It was launched on the third day of the mission, orbited in

In the months of training before the flight, I had not gotten the actual feeling of going into space. The real thing was incredible.

—Ellen Ochoa

Ochoa joined fellow astronauts Kenneth Cameron (bottom, left), mission commander; C. Michael Foale, mission specialist (next to Cameron); Stephen S. Oswald, pilot (middle back); and Kenneth D. Cockrell, mission specialist aboard the space shuttle Discovery's *aft flight deck for a traditional photo before liftoff from Johnson Space Center, Houston, Texas, in 1993.* (Courtesy National Aeronautics and Space Administration)

space for two days on its own, and then was picked up again by the shuttle.

The shuttle's crew collected information about the Sun's corona, the bright ring of gases and particles around the Sun; the corona can be seen during a solar eclipse, when the Sun's light is obscured by the Moon moving between the Sun and Earth. The crew also measured the speed of the Sun's particles that fall into Earth's atmosphere. Ochoa and the rest of the crew did their work without any difficulty, and in fact, there were no problems either with the vehicle or in space.

"Space flight is a great experience!" Ochoa recalled.

> In orbit, unbuckled from the launch harness and with our helmet removed, there is a sense of weightlessness. It's strange, but you get used to it. You grow an inch or two (2.5 to 5 cm) in near-zero gravity, because the discs between the vertebrae of the back are no longer pushed down by gravity. Your waist even gets smaller and your legs thinner.

Even ordinary things like eating are different in space. Food is either dehydrated or freeze-dried and come from a small dispenser. There are no bathing or shower facilities, so shuttle crews take sponge baths at a personal hygiene station. There is, however, a small bathroom with a window that gives an out-of-this-world view. Looking at Earth from space is very special.

Shuttle mission STS-56 lasted nine days, six hours, and nine minutes. It made 148 orbits around Earth and landed at the Kennedy Space Center in Florida on April 17.

"When I was traveling in space, I thought about how lucky I was to be up there and how so many people would want to have the job that I have," Ochoa said. "I was glad to go into space, and do my job. But I was glad to get back on Earth, too!"

Ochoa made a second trip into space as payload commander on the *Atlantis,* as a member of the STS-66 Atmospheric Laboratory for Applications and Science-3 (ATLAS-3) mission from November 3

Ochoa checks out a 35mm camera before taking pictures on Discovery's *flight deck. She and four other astronauts spent nine days in space supporting the Atlas 2 mission in 1993.* (Courtesy National Aeronautics and Space Administration)

> *The first two minutes of liftoff are the most dangerous, as the rockets build up to incredible thrust and speed.*
>
> —Ellen Ochoa

to 14, 1994. ATLAS-3 continued the series of spacelab flights to study the energy of the Sun during an 11-year solar cycle and to learn how changes in the Sun's irradiance (radiant energy) affect Earth's climate and environment.

Shuttle mission STS-66 was another phase of a continuing study of how Earth's environment is changing and how human beings affect that change. Part of the shuttle's payload included cages with 10 pregnant rats and equipment to monitor the effects of space flight on them. Experiments in this part of the mission were on behalf of the National Institutes of Health to provide insights into the fields of gravitational and space biology and gravity's effects on living organisms.

Payload commander on the space shuttle Atlantis *in 1994, Ochoa can be seen here completing an operation at the controls for the Remote Manipulator System arm, working beside Donald McMonagle, mission commander.* (Courtesy National Aeronautics and Space Administration)

Ochoa, an accomplished flutist, took a brief time out from a busy day in space to play a 15-minute set of flute selections on the space shuttle Discovery *in 1993.* (Courtesy National Aeronautics and Space Administration)

Ochoa's main assignment on the mission was to retrieve the CRISTA-SPAS atmospheric research satellite at the end of its eight-day free flight. She again used a remote retrieving arm to accomplish this.

Besides her research work in optics and robotics to further the success of the space program, Ochoa spends a great deal of time and energy speaking to young people at schools all over the country, encouraging them to get a good education and pursue their career dreams. She tries especially to be a role model for young girls and Hispanics, telling them that if they study hard and reach far enough, they can achieve any goal they desire. "Stay in school," she encourages young people. "Education increases career options and gives you a chance for a wide variety of jobs. If you want to be an astronaut, get a college degree in a technical field such as science, math, or medicine. Either work for NASA or join one of the military services to learn more and work more in your chosen specialty."

Ochoa has her private pilot's license and, in training for space missions, flies "back seat" in T-38 aircraft. She also is an accomplished musician, a classical flutist, and for recreation she enjoys playing volleyball and bicycling.

Since her second shuttle flight, Ochoa's main work for NASA has been in two major areas—robotics and space station research and development. She is a crew representative for robotics development, testing, and training. As part of NASA's role in the International Space Station program, she is an assistant to the chief of the Astronaut Office, directing crew involvement in the development and operation of the station. In this work she has been part of teams representing NASA at many conferences in Russia and other foreign countries on the advancement of space station technology.

"As for the future, I'd like to go on more shuttle missions and also work on a space station," Ochoa said. "It would be exciting to live in a space habitat and help keep its operating system going, using resources already there such as fuel. I'd also love to go to the Moon, or Mars."

Chronology

MAY 10, 1958	Ellen Ochoa is born in Los Angeles, California
1975	graduates from Grossmont High School, La Mesa, California
1980	is valedictorian of graduating class and receives bachelor of science degree in physics from San Diego State University
1981	receives master of science degree from Stanford University on an engineering fellowship
1985	receives doctorate in electrical engineering from Stanford University on another fellowship and joins Sandia National Laboratories, Livermore, California
1988	joins NASA's Ames Research Center at Moffett Field, California
1990	is selected by NASA to begin astronaut training; marries Coe Fulmer Miles
1991	becomes an astronaut
1993	joins crew of *Discovery* shuttle on mission STS-56 as mission specialist for nine-day space flight to conduct atmospheric and solar studies
1994	joins crew of *Atlantis* shuttle on mission STS-66 as mission specialist for 11-day space flight to conduct atmospheric and solar studies
1994–PRESENT	works for NASA in robotics and space station research and development; serves as assistant to chief of Astronaut Office in international space station development and operation program

Further Reading

Books and Information about Ellen Ochoa

Dunn, Wendy, and Janet Morey. *Famous Hispanic Americans.* New York: Dutton/Cobblehill Books, 1996. Includes brief biography of Ochoa.

Kamp, Jim, and Diane Telgen. *Notable Hispanic American Women.* Detroit: Gale, 1995. Adult book with short biography of Ochoa that is not too scientific.

McMurray, Emily J. *Notable Twentieth-Century Scientists.* Detroit: Gale, 1995. Adult book with short biography of Ochoa that is not too technical.

NASA Johnson Space Center. "Biographical Data—Ellen Ochoa." NASA Johnson Space Center, Houston (September 1996). Biographical information.

————. "Missions Highlights STS-56." NASA Johnson Space Center, Houston (May 1993). Descriptions of shuttle missions.

Books and Videos on Related Topics

Living in Space. Houston, NASA Teacher Resource Center. 1997 videotape of U.S. astronauts on space shuttle missions. Available from NASA Teacher Resource Center, Johnson Space Center, Houston, TX 77058.

Ride, Sally, and Tam O'Shaughnessy. *Voyager: An Adventure to the Edge of the Solar System.* New York: Crown, 1992. America's first woman astronaut describes her adventure into outer space in an exciting book for young adults.

Verba, Joan Marie. *Voyager: Exploring the Outer Planets.* Minneapolis: Lerner, 1991. Young adult book on NASA's Voyager missions.

Go online to download NASA's biography of Ellen Ochoa and get detailed descriptions about her two space flights. The address of the Ellen Ochoa World Wide Web Site is http://www.jsc.nasa.gov/bios/htmlbios/ochoa.html.

Index

Numbers in *italics* indicate illustrations. Numbers in **boldface** indicate main topics.

A

agriculture and agroforestry 33, 40
  Sánchez's work in 33–44, *34, 39*
Aldrin, Edwin, Jr. 13
Alonso, Isabel 25
Alvarez, Luis *vii,* **1–12,** *7, 9*
  chronology 10–11
  death 10, 11
  education 3–4, 10
  further reading 11–12
  marriage and children 4, 8, 10, 11
Alvarez, Walter 2, 4, 8, *9*
Alvarez: Adventures of a Physicist (Alvarez) 1, 3, 10
Argentina 29–30
Argonne Laboratories 5, 11
Armstrong, Neil 13
Asaro, Frank *9*
astronauts 13, *14,* 17, *110*

Ellen Ochoa *106,* 107–16, *110, 111, 112, 113*
Atlantis 111–12, *112,* 115
Atlas 2 111
atom 4
atomic bomb 1–2, 5–6, 9–10, 11
atomic energy 4

B

Baez, Albert vi
Bandy, Dale 38
Batista, Fulgencio 58
Baylor College of Medicine 16, 18–19, 21
Berkeley, University of California at 4, 6, *7,* 11
biodiversity 72, 74, *75,* 76, 78
Brown University 27, 30, 31

bubble chambers *viii,* 3, 6, *7*
Buenos Aires 29–30
Buol, Stanley 36, 37

C

California, University of
  at Berkeley 4, 6, *7,* 11
  at Irvine 50, 53
California Institute of Technology (CalTech), Jet Propulsion Laboratory (JPL) at 50, 51, 54, *82,* 83–85, 89, 90, 91
California State Department of Water Resources 97
Cameron, Kenneth *110*
Campbell, Joseph 65
cardiology 16, 17, 18, 19
Cardona, Manuel **23–32,** *24, 27, 28*
  awards 29, 31, 32

chronology 31–32
education 26, 31
further reading 32
marriage and children
27, 31
Cardús, David **13–22**, *14,*
18
awards 20, 22
chronology 21–22
education 15–16, 21
further reading 22
marriage and children
16, 21
societies 20
Castro, Fidel 58
Caudle, Neil 37
Central University of Venezuela 71, 80
centrifuge 17–18
Chang-Díaz, Franklin vi
Chevron Corporation *94,*
97–98, 100, 101, 104
Chicxulub 89
chlorofluorocarbons
(CFCs) 49–50, 51, 52
civil engineering 97
Clinton, Bill 51, 54, 101
Cockrell, Kenneth D. *110*
Colorado State University
(CSU) 72, 73, 80
Colmenares, Margarita *94,*
95–105, *99, 102*
chronology 104
education 95–97,
102–3, 104
further reading 105
honors and awards 103
Columbia 108
Comisión Femenil 90
Comiskey, James A. 76
Compton, Arthur 3
computers 26
in medicine 17, 18–19,
20
conservationism *68,* 69, 78
Crutzen, Paul 51, 54

Cuba 35, 57–58

D

Dallmeier, Francisco *68,*
69–81, *73, 75, 77, 79*
chronology 80–81
education 71, 72, 73
further reading 81
marriage and children
72–73, 80
deforestation 33, *34*
Díaz, Henry **56–67**, *57,*
61, 63
chronology 65–66
education 59, 60, 65
further reading 66–67
marriage and children
59, 60, 64, 65
dinosaurs 2, 9, 11, 89
Discovery mission 107,
109–11, *110, 111, 113,*
115

E

Education, U.S. Depart-
ment of *94,* 101, 103, 104
Egypt 8, 11
Eisenhower, Dwight D. 9
electrical engineering 108
Ochoa's work in *106,*
107–16
electronics 23, *24*
elementary particles 6
*El Niño: Historical and Pa-
leoclimatic Aspects of the
Southern Oscillation* (Díaz)
61, 66
El Niño/Southern Oscilla-
tion (ENSO) 57, *57,*
62–64, *63*
engineering 97
electrical 108
electrical, Ochoa's work
in *106,* 107–16

environmental, Col-
menares's work in *94,*
95–105
Society of Hispanic Pro-
fessional Engineers
89–90, 98–99, 100,
101, 104
Enola Gay 1, 5
environmental chemistry,
Molina's work in 45–55,
46
environmental engineering,
Colmenares's work in *94,*
95–105
ephemeris 85
Escalante, Jaime vi
European Space Agency 89
exercise physiology 17, 18

F

farming and forestry 33, 40
Sánchez's work in
33–44, *34, 39*
Fermi, Enrico 5, 11
Foale, C. Michael *110*
*Forest Biodiversity Research,
Monitoring, and Modeling*
(Dallmeier and Comiskey,
eds.) 76, 81
forest inventories 74–76
Franco, Francisco 15, 26
Friesen, Sten von 6–8

G

Galileo 86–88, *86, 87, 88,*
91
Garriga, Miguel 25
General Electric 97
germanium 25, 26, 27, 28
Glaser, Donald 6
gravity 110, 112
artificial 17, *18*
Gutiérrez, Orlando vi

H

Haller, E. E. 29
Hermes mission 89, 91
Hiroshima 1, 2, 5, 11
hurricanes 56, 58–59
hydrogen bomb 6

I

International Centre for Research in Agroforestry (ICRAF) 40
International Congress of Physical Medicine and Rehabilitation 19
Introduction to Mathematics for Physicians and Biologists, An (Cardús) 19
iridium 8
Irvine, University of California at 50, 53

J

Japan 90
Jet Propulsion Laboratory (JPL), CalTech 50, 51, 54, *82,* 83–85, 89, 90, 91
Jupiter 86–88, *86, 87, 88*

K

Kearns, David 101
Kefren, pyramid of 8, 11
K-electron capture 4
Kennedy, John F. 8, 11
Kenya 40, 41

L

LaSalle Museum of Natural History 71, 80
Lawrence, Ernest Orlando 4
Loero, Domingo 37

Lovelace Foundation 17, 21

M

Manhattan Project 5
Mars 83–84, 85, 91
    Observer Project 85, 91
Massachusetts Institute of Technology (MIT) 5, 11, 51, 54
mathematical models, in medicine 17, 18–19
Max Planck Institute of Solid-State Physics 27, 28, 30, 31
McCants, Charles 37
McMonagle, Donald *112*
medicine, Cardús's work in 13–22, *14*
Mercury 89, 91
meteorology 59–60
    Díaz's work in 56–67, *57, 61, 63*
Mexico 89, 90
Michel, Helen *9*
Molina, Felipe 50, 51
Molina, Mario **45–55,** *46, 52*
    chronology 53–54
    education 47–48, 53
    further reading 54–55
    marriage 48, 50, 51, 53
Moon 13

N

Nagasaki 2
National Aeronautics and Space Administration (NASA) 13, 17, *18,* 83, 84–85, 89, 90, 91, 92, 101, 108, 109, 114, 115
    Discovery mission 107, 109–11, *110, 111, 113,* 115

Galileo mission 86–88, *86, 87, 88,* 91
    shuttle missions *82, 106,* 107, 108, 109–14, 115
National Oceanic and Atmospheric Administration (NOAA) 60, 61, 65, 66
Near-Infrared Mapping Spectrometer (NIMS) 86, 87–88, *88*
Nobel, Alfred vi, 2
Nobel Prize vi, *viii,* 1, 3, 4, 5, 6, 11, 45, *46,* 51, 54
North Carolina State University (NCSU) 36, 37, 39, 40, 42–43
No Universal Constants: Journeys of Women in Science and Engineering (Ambrose, ed.) 96
Novello, Antonia vi

O

Ocampo, Adriana *82,* **83–93,** *86, 87, 88*
    awards 90
    chronology 91–92
    education 84–85, 90, 91
    further reading 92–93
    marriage 91
Ochoa, Ellen *106,* **107–16,** *110, 111, 112, 113*
    chronology 115
    education 108, 115
    further reading 116
    marriage 109, 115
optical spectroscopy 26
optics, in robotics *106,* 109
Oswald, Lee Harvey 8
Oswald, Stephen S. *110*
ozone pollution *46,* 48–50, 51

P

paraplegics 17, 18
particle accelerators 6
particle physics 6–8, 11
Pascual, Pedro 27
Pathfinder 83–84
Peru 34–35, 36–39,
    42–43, 69–70
physics 23
    Alvarez's work viii, 1–12
    Cardona's work 23–32,
        24
    particle 6–8, 11
    solid-state 23–25, 24,
        29, 30, 32
planetary geology 84
    Ocampo's work in
        83–93
Planetary Society, The 89
plutonium bomb 5
Properties and Management
    of Soils of the Tropics
    (Sánchez) 40
Public Health Service, U.S.
    16

R

radar 2, 5
rain forests 74
rehabilitation medicine 17,
    18, 19, 21
Rice University 16, 19
Ride, Sally 108
Romero, Juan Carlos vi
Rowland, F. "Sherry" Sher-
    wood 48, 49, 50, 51, 52,
    54

S

Sánchez, Pedro 33–44, 34,
    39, 41
    awards 41
    chronology 42–43
    education 35, 36, 42

further reading 43–44
    marriage and children
        36, 40, 42, 43
    societies 40–41
semiconductors 25, 26,
    29, 31
Sherbrook University 28
shuttle missions 82, 106,
    107, 108, 109–14, 115
    Discovery 107, 109–11,
        110, 111, 113, 115
silicon 25, 26, 27, 28
silicon chips 25
slash-and-burn farming 33
Smithsonian Institution
    73–74, 75, 80
Society of Hispanic Profes-
    sional Engineers (SHPE)
    90, 98–99, 100, 101, 104
soil science, Sánchez's work
    in 33–44, 34, 39
solid-state physics 23–25,
    24, 29, 30, 32
Space Conference for the
    Americas: Prospects in Co-
    operation 89, 91
space program 13, 16, 17,
    83–90, 108, 114
    Discovery mission 107,
        109–11, 110, 111, 113,
        115
    shuttle missions 82,
        106, 107, 108, 109–14,
        115
Spanish Civil War 15,
    25–26, 27
Spencer, William A. 19
superconductors 25, 26,
    28, 32

T

Tapia, Richard vi
telecommunications
    19–20, 26
transistors 25, 26

Tree Watch 76, 80
tritium 5, 11
tropical areas 33, 34, 74

U

United Nations 89
U.S. Department of Educa-
    tion 94, 101, 103, 104
U.S. Public Health Service
    16

V

Venezuela 71–72, 80
Viking mission 85
Voyager mission 85

W

wavelength 4–5
weather 56–57
    Díaz's work 56–67, 57,
        61, 63
    El Niño 57, 57, 62–64,
        63
    meteorology 59–60
White House fellowships
    101, 104
Whitman, Walt v
Wiens, Jake 4
wildlife biology 72
    Dallmeier's work in 68,
        69–81
World War II 2, 5–6,
    9–10, 26, 27

X

Xerox 96, 101

Y

Yurimaguas 36–39